# Christmas
## Will Forever Be
# Your
# Season

*Every Lover Leaves an Everlasting Mark: A Memoir*

# Mo Melo

Book Cover and Illustrations by Mitxeran
Edited by Calley Overton
Proofread by Liz Saucedo
Layout by Manuel Quintana

First paperback edition: August, 2023
Paperback: 979-8-218-23908-4
E-book: 979-8-218-23909-1

Instagram: MoMeloChristmas
Tiktok: MoMeloChristmas
www.momelochristmas.com

Love is like a myth.
There is some truth and some fantasy but, most importantly,
its core is surrounded by what could have been, the potential
it could have had, and what should have been.
Like our story.

# New Endings

I don't know what's wrong with me, but I'm rarely single.

I'm one of those people who—as soon as they break up with someone—always have others wondering, "How long will it be until they find themselves in another relationship?" and the bets start rolling in.

To me, life is more beautiful when shared with someone you love. The memories you create together will always be more powerful. Watching a movie is a completely different experience if you have another person by your side, laughing with you and airing their thoughts. A boring trip to a train museum can suddenly become exciting if you have the right person next to you.

If people say that sharing is caring, sharing a life with someone you love is the ultimate goal.

It hasn't always been like that for me, though. It all started at eighteen when I moved out of my small town in Portugal to go to college. I was excited to finally live without my parents in my country's capital, Lisbon, where I could express my sexuality without objections or fear. Up to that point, I had been too afraid of sharing with anyone who I was. *Gay.* That word terrified me so much that I could never say it when I was younger. Word travels fast in a small town, and soon enough, my parents would know about my true identity, and I was scared they would kick me out of the house or stop acknowledging my existence. Because of that, for the longest time, I hid who I was from them. It was only when I moved to New York City that I told them about who I really was. The result was tears, sadness, and five years where it was a forbidden topic of conversation.

When I moved to college, it took me less than one month to start dating my first boyfriend. After him, the "never single" cycle started, and it never stopped.

There was always a person I was seeing or a relationship going on. The longest I have been single was around nine months and that was because of COVID. There was something in me that said I couldn't enjoy life if I didn't have someone by my side. Not having a partner meant that I was failing in life, especially in those times when all my friends were getting engaged.

Things are different nowadays. Since my last breakup, I haven't had the desire to date anyone. For the first time, I'm actually mourning the loss of a relationship instead of jumping into a replacement.

Sometimes a shorter relationship can have the most significant impact on you. It isn't about how long two people are together, but how much you learn and grow from the experience, and surprisingly, this love story taught me a lot about myself.

Toward the end, I could feel the relationship fading, but I was unsure why. It was clear that we both cared for one another, and I didn't want to lose what we had been building. It made no sense. I started to overcompensate since the distance made me feel anxious and sad. I did everything I could, but in the end, I did end up losing him.

I also lost myself in the process, but ultimately, I mourned someone for the first time in my life.

This is the story of the lessons I learned when I allowed myself to grieve someone without trying to replace them right away.

# Step One:

# Denial

Day One

*Hey, today I saw one of those Hallmark movies you enjoy so much and I thought of you.*

It's interesting how you believe in the concept of *the one*, also known as the existence of a Prince Charming. You two will meet one day, and soon after, he will sweep you off your feet. You will realize you have everything in common, a match made in heaven, without a single flaw in sight.

Well . . . reality is different. It isn't a perfect replica of that vision. If you keep running away from conflict, deciding to disappear at the first difficulty, afraid that the existence of a problem will shatter this illusion, I have bad news for you. Throughout life, you will constantly be lying to yourself, saying that the prince in front of you is not so charming and therefore is definitely not *the one*. We need to understand that conflict is a natural part of any relationship, and it's how we deal with it that defines the strength of the relationship.

Yet, I forgive you. I don't think our differences were that big; you were just scared of commitment. Given what had happened to you in the past, you decided that it was easier to push me away than to be vulnerable. This way, you would protect yourself from ever being hurt again in the future. Although it hurts me, I understand.

You don't have to worry. I'll be alright. I have always been a fighter. I'm known to never give up on the ones I love.

In fact, I had the most brilliant idea ever. Since you love Hallmark movies, you already know that the main couple always finds an issue that prevents their love from moving on. This is the moment where the main character's love interest finds a way to do the most outrageous romantic thing ever and redeem themselves in the eyes of the love of their life. In other words, since my life feels like a Hallmark movie right now, the simple thing I need to do to win you back is a grand love gesture! Easy! Soon, our lives will be intertwined, and I will be happy again.

The first step is finding out what you like the most (which is the easiest part because I know you well). You love Hallmark movies, and your number one love language is words of affirmation.

Unfortunately, I have always struggled with your preferred love language. Throughout my life, words have been empty promises from my exes, promises of changed behavior that never happened. Because of that, I always disregarded them.

If you were to compliment me, I would always feel like an imposter when I returned the favor. It would feel insincere and disingenuous. Sometimes, I would force myself to say something nice to you because it mattered to you, but it never sounded natural to me. It felt like I was reading a script without feeling any emotion. Giving you a hug from behind was my preferred way of saying *I love you* or even a kiss on the forehead. To you, expressing love meant saying the most romantic thing imaginable.

Nonetheless, if I want to win you back, I need to overcome my insecurities. I have to write the most beautiful bunch of letters that scream *I LOVE YOU AND I WANT YOU BACK.*

This won't be an easy mission, as I'm not a writer or a poet. In fact, English isn't my first language, and sometimes I struggle with it. Whenever you misunderstood something I said, you would try to make me feel better by joking about it. You would say that, although you were fluent in English, you barely spoke the language sometimes. On the other hand, my first (and hopefully only) ex-husband would make fun of my broken English. He stated that my inability to pronounce the *th* sound would have people label me as a baby, which would lead me to never be taken seriously. That's to say, my self-esteem wasn't the best to embark on this project. I tortured myself with the question: *Would I be able to articulate my thoughts well enough?*

Against all odds, as soon as I destroyed that memory and tried to tackle the challenging mission of writing a book, I discovered that words came naturally to me! I often felt the need to write down my thoughts, capturing them in these pages. These words are beautiful and true. They are *my* truth. They are *our* story.

I could have texted you these thoughts in the form of one thousand love letters instead. You would wake up every single day to the most beautiful good morning text you have ever seen in your life. Maybe you would brand me as exhausting and crazy, but that's what love is, right? It's that scene in those romance movies that always wins the protagonist back. It's the perfect combination of desperation, love, craziness, romance, and perseverance.

The reality is, if I had texted you those feelings—even once—I would have grown anxious thinking about when you would read them. The heartbreak of being left on *delivered* would have been unbearable. I don't want to go through the experience of waiting for a response for days and days because there probably won't be one. That pain would be too real. I can't go through it again. If I was already impatient when I didn't get a morning message before work, imagine the anxiety I would feel if you never replied to the most important message I had ever written: *I love you and I want you back.*

I believe that one day the hopeless romantic in you would wander into a bookstore and pick up this very book feeling intrigued. I envisioned that you would be drawn to the title because you adored Christmas like no one else. Our time spent together during the holiday season was so magical and special that I will think of you and what we shared every year when Christmas comes.

After reading the title, you would likely read the author's name out loud: Mo Melo. It would bring some unfamiliar comfort to you because it sounds like *cogumelo*, one of your favorite words in my native language. The definition of it only means *mushroom*, but that word also meant a smile on your face whenever you would pronounce it. There would be this enigmatic aura to this name that would awaken your curiosity, even without realizing that the last name is a very common one in my home country and that the first name, Mo, is short for Gizmo.

It might be a strange pick, but *Gremlins* was one of the first movies we saw together. We called it a Christmas movie for the sake of being festive and held hands while watching the cutest gremlin save the day. Many days after that date, when you saw a big surprise I had prepared for you, you turned to me, with the most speechless look possible, and said, "You're a Gizmo in a sea of gremlins." Although that might sound unappealing to a lot of people, it was the sweetest thing you could have said at that moment.

I fantasize you will buy this book without knowing that you will end up thinking of me. I dream that reading this story, revisiting the memories of what we had, and thinking about our laughs together will bring back our love.

Then, you would see the story we could have shared together. Maybe, at that moment, you will think that this is the most romantic act in the history of the world and decide to message me.

That's my mission because I care about you. If I didn't, I couldn't say that every Christmas to come will be a painful reminder of you.

*Hey, do you still remember the day we met online?*

I will never forget the day I felt the need to go back to dating apps. I got that weird feeling after a breakup when you don't know if you're ready to date again but, at the same time, you want to.

People usually say that the best way to forget an ex-lover is to start chatting with new people, and I had that thought stuck in my head for a while. I love the idea of love, of being in a relationship, of having someone, but I was unsure if I had fully healed from my previous ex. The breakup was a done deal with no chance of getting back together, and I wondered if anyone ever fully heals from heartbreak.

After taking a few deep breaths, also known as redownloading the dating app Hinge. I decided that getting to know someone new would be the best way for me to fully move on.

Unfortunately, the guys that I saw on the app weren't impressive, and I thought it was probably time to delete my old profile and start a new one. I had been using my account on Hinge for four years, but I had changed a lot since I first created that profile.

For instance, I had grown facial hair. A beard changes your whole look, and who knows what the algorithm knew about me. Starting from scratch would be the best way to find out. Forget what you know about me—I have grown, and so has my face. Now show me the men!

As I was deciding whether to delete it or not, I stumbled upon your profile. There you were with a charming smirk, the first profile that made me stop to admire it carefully.

I went through your profile, and I could only think of how attractive you were. Everything appeared to be perfect, until your height was disclosed. This was a problem. I tend to like taller guys. There are no words to explain how I adore hugging someone, resting my head on their chest or shoulder, and that feeling of coziness and protection. My height is very average, so it isn't that hard to find someone taller. However, you were only two inches taller than me. Plus, if you were lying about it—as most guys do—there was the possibility that I could be taller than you.

I questioned myself if I should stop there and skip your profile. The truth was that I found the rest of the profile to be intriguing which made it a hard decision, but I ended up choosing to give it another chance and keep investigating.

As I scrolled to the bottom of your profile, I came across this stupid line. Upon being asked what you were into, you replied, "neurotic little weirdos." How could someone have described me so well? Had I found someone who shared my sense of humor? Would everything be fine and height not be a big issue at the end of the day?

I decided I had to take a chance at destiny and send you a like. I just had to find the best conversation starter so I wouldn't blend in with the crowd. Luckily, you had this line on your profile that intrigued me. You were describing your obsession with Diet Coke, and I used it as the perfect opportunity to send a message: *How many cans of Diet Coke are in your fridge right now?*

When I hit the send button, I felt proud of my clever icebreaker as I couldn't believe the interesting coincidence that was happening. I was relaxing on a friend's couch, and he had an incredible obsession with Coke Zero, your archnemesis. He and I often joked that the worst type of addict was a Coke Zero drinker since their fridge would always be at least half stocked with this drink.

Shortly after, I set my phone down, as the next guys weren't my cup of tea. I wish I could make a terrible pun and say that they weren't my cup of soda, but this neurotic little weirdo will refrain himself from making it.

We matched a few days later and panic took over me. Up until that point, the thoughts about deleting the app and starting fresh had been growing and growing. I had only sent a handful of likes and my expectations about getting a match were practically none. I wasn't counting on one until you proved me wrong. Now, I had an excuse to stick around a little bit longer. Thankfully, I did.

As we sent messages back and forth, we soon discovered we had so many similar interests. To my surprise, you had even

studied my native language in college. It was only for a semes-
ter, but it was still impressive!

Everything about you was purely fascinating. You were so
captivating that you were the only person I was talking with. I
mean, you were also the only match I had since I didn't want
to create a new profile. Not at that point. Only after meeting
you in person would I entertain that thought.

I was afraid, I'm not going to deny it. I didn't know if
it was still too early after my last relationship. Unfortunately,
there is never an answer or recipe for how, or when, to heal a
broken heart.

That's why I usually rely on my friends for their validation
and encouragement. They are the best people to tell me the
truth—if they think I'm ready or not. If they tell me, "You
have been too desperate and on edge lately. This isn't the best
time to date," maybe I should listen.

So, one night, at a local bar that my friends and I visit
weekly, I asked them for their opinion after showing them your
profile. I told them I wanted to meet you to see what would
come out of it, however, I was too nervous to ask you out. I
didn't fear rejection. I was just nervous. I wanted to make sure
I was ready; otherwise, I would waste a great opportunity simply because I rushed things.

To my surprise, all my friends told me you looked like a
catch and that there was no reason for me not to leave the
hesitation outside the door. They didn't see you as a rebound
guy, and they assured me that I should pursue you.

That small pep talk made me feel better. I felt more confident about my decision to keep getting to know you. If my friends don't think I'm an emotional wreck, why shouldn't I trust them?

When I woke up the next morning, I received a message from you asking me out on a date.

How was that possible? It felt like divine intervention. One minute I was asking for guidance from my friends, and the next, the universe was telling me that it was time to move forward.

Little did I know that it would be the beginning of a beautiful love story.

*Hey, did the day we met change you as well?*

What a first date we had! We agreed to meet up for lunch at a vegan restaurant because you were vegetarian, and I had no preferences when it came to food. It was one of the first days of fall, still warm, but you could feel the cold weather slowly creeping in. I opted to walk to the restaurant to bask in the last days of sunshine while talking with my mother on the phone. Our conversation had a significant impact on me since it was the first time I had told her about going out on a date.

It felt liberating to finally be able to talk with my parents about my love life, given that they always struggled with my homosexuality. She did have too many questions about my preference for deciding to go on a date with a man and not a woman. She was still learning. While trying to answer her questions, I warned her that I had just gotten to the restaurant and that I had been the first one to arrive. That meant that I would have to hang up on her as soon as you walked through the door.

Then the most heavy-hitting question came up: *Why was I not trying to date women as well?* She thought I could potentially meet a woman who was the love of my life and it would be the easiest way to start a family. I understood this wasn't the

17

best conversation to have before a date. I didn't want to start it feeling defeated, once again thinking that I couldn't get my mother's approval. Luckily, I saw you right away, and I quickly hung up on her.

I was in disbelief. I can't describe the shock I experienced when you walked through that door wearing a button-up shirt, ready to impress me. Your smile was captivating. Your energy was so comforting. Somehow your voice was even more charming than I had imagined. I was in awe. You were more attractive than in those photos, and I felt like the luckiest man alive when we greeted each other with a hug.

It's so fascinating how quickly we bonded. How two indecisive people made the waitress pick out the meals that we later shared. That quirky server was the perfect stabilizer for the two flames dancing between us. She was new to the job, and it was the ideal gateway for us to start talking about something other than how windy it was outside. But it wasn't like we needed an excuse to communicate because we kept talking and talking until we finished our meals. We felt the pressure to leave that restaurant and free up the table, but at the same time, we also felt like we still had the world to talk about. That's why we decided to keep the date going and head to a bar.

There was a nearby bar with arcade machines against the walls that you had been wanting to visit for a while, and I was more than happy to oblige. Inside, I made you try my sour beer, my favorite style that you weren't familiar with. After you took a sip, you looked me in the eyes. I expected to hear your thoughts on it, but you pulled me in for a kiss instead. You had been dying to do that the whole date. At first, I felt like it might have been a little bit rushed but, oh damn . . .

I surrendered myself to your lips and embraced the way the kiss made me feel. So good. It felt so unique. Your lips wrapped around mine. Your hand around my waist while we blocked the path to the arcades. As if everyone was a mere random character in our own game. It was *our* time.

Although we were that obnoxious couple constantly making out in the most annoying place imaginable, that thought didn't bother us. It felt like two missing puzzle pieces finally encountering each other and marveling at how well they fit inside one another. If time had frozen when I saw you walk into the restaurant, I should thank it for being so gracious for freezing twice that day. The way you had pulled my hips toward your body, dying to know how my lips tasted, was magnetic. It was one of those kisses you wish everyone gets to experience once in their lifetime. That kiss that pulls you in, making you tremble inside, making you fantasize about waking up every single day for the rest of your life to that feeling. If forever meant waking up to that for as long as we lived, I would pray for the existence of an afterlife so I could transform it into eternity.

It didn't take us long to realize we weren't playing that many arcade games. We would play one here and there, in between conversations and kisses. Because of that, we decided to go to a different bar, one where we could sit down and talk in peace. That was when I started getting nervous. Uncertainty is such a crushing burden, and the thought of the possibility of us running out of topics to talk about was devastating. It would be the realization that all that promise and potential was just a mere spark. Lust. That there was no substance after that kiss. What if our date was a waste of time because we lacked compatibility? We were just kissing one another to fill the void since we didn't know what else to talk about.

On our way out, I got cold when the wind started picking up. My head hadn't wrapped around the concept that fall was starting and I needed to bring warmer jackets. I shivered, and you took that as the perfect opportunity to put your arm around me once again. On the pretext that it was to warm me up, I accepted it. I felt so comfortable around you. I also noticed our height difference when I saw you struggle to put your arm around my shoulders. Those two inches separating us really made things more complicated. I didn't mind it, though; I appreciated you using any excuse you could find to get closer to me. Disguised as being altruistic, you could put your arm around me anytime you liked.

We kept walking together with your arm around me like we had known each other for years. We had an unmatched chemistry that would never reveal that we had just met. And I realized we were still talking. When the conversation started to die, a new topic would emerge. I was captivated by you.

All that self-doubt was idiotic. It was me trying to sabotage what we had because I thought it was too perfect to be true. I needed to embrace the magic of the present moment instead of thinking about the worst-case scenario. I had a charming guy hugging me and trying to keep me warm against the cold wind. At that moment, I had everything I could ever wish for.

We made it to a dive bar because there is no better place for two souls who simply want to connect at every possible level than a bar that will have no judgments. Perhaps there would already be a couple making out in a dark corner, possibly on their first date as well. We sat by the bar to force our mouths to stay away from temptation. To focus on just talking.

That was when I discovered your love for bad Hallmark movies and how excited you were that Christmas was coming. The season brought you so much joy and happiness. You loved seeing all the decorations, all the lights, the spirit of it, and those cheesy Hallmark Christmas movies. You were another hopeless romantic soul desperate for love. While I didn't like romantic movies because of their unrealistic nature, for you, it was the opposite. You loved them for how cheesy and romantic they were—the stupidity of it all amazed you.

They say that opposites attract; we had different views on a topic that led me to speak about what was on my mind. My truest thought. My one desire. All I wanted was to cuddle with you and watch one of those movies with you. The reality was that I hadn't seen any Hallmark movies, but seeing your eyes sparkle when you started talking about them was magical. You were so passionate that all I wanted to do was understand their magic. With you. I wanted to feel your body next to mine on a couch as we watched one-and-a-half hours of a crazy, unrealistic love story set at Christmas.

Luckily, time wasn't on our side that day, which may have been for the best, or we would have ended up rushing things. Even if we did have more time, I still feel like you would have pulled the brakes on my impulsive behavior, as you always did it so well. Somehow, that night, the lack of time didn't stop us from going to a third bar to talk even more. We must have spent a total of six to eight hours just talking and laughing, with some kissing in between. To me, that was the beginning of my Christmas miracle. It had been a date for the books, pun intended.

When I got home after a long but beautiful day, I saw you had sent me your phone number on Hinge. I was over the moon knowing you had also enjoyed getting to know me in person. I felt complete. I also wondered how many more little quirks I would find about your personality and how many new ways I would find to fall in love with you.

I hope you still feel the same way about that first date. I hope that upon reading this, you will relive that day and realize how extraordinary it was. That we were meant for each other. That this separation was a mistake. I hope time has reserved a special place for us to reunite because all I desire is for us to meet again and have everything go back to what it was.

*Hey, I listened to our song again today.*

I thought that hanging out with some friends all day long would be the best solution to try to push your memory away from my mind. I figured I wouldn't think about you if I kept myself busy every second of the day. It would be impossible. It had to be. I also figured that lying to myself would be easier. I told myself that if I kept myself permanently occupied, I wouldn't be sad. Today was a reassurance that I'm the world's most terrible liar.

You were special to me. You meant so much to me that the thought of you constantly finds a way to slip into my mind, catching me in the most unexpected places and moments. The simple sight of something that reminds me of you can bring back all those sweet memories. That's what happened today.

When I was on my way home—trying to accept the fact that my friends were gone and that I was finally alone with my thoughts—I quickly decided to listen to music so I could silence them, going back to a protective bubble where you couldn't reach me.

Besides not knowing what to order at a restaurant, I never know what playlist or album to select on Spotify either. There is beauty in every option. My friends blame my indecisiveness on my zodiac sign (I'm a Libra), especially the one who is coincidentally a ginger Leo. There are actually two, but I won't say which one as I'm sure they will fight for the spotlight.

That's why I randomly picked *USA Hot Hits*, thinking I would hear upbeat songs. I needed to listen to the type of music that makes people happy and want to dance. But then, despite being mixed with such a long list of tracks, our song started playing. My bubble exploded. I was petrified, and I could no longer run away from my feelings.

The most interesting part is that you didn't know that I considered it to be our song. I wonder if back then you had a song that reminded you of me. A song that still makes you think of me. Every couple has "their song," whether it was playing when they first met or when they first kissed. Or maybe it was just the number one song when they started dating. Our song holds a special meaning to me for a different reason.

When we were together, I had traveled to my hometown to celebrate Christmas with my family, and on my way back from this trip, I felt a level of happiness I hadn't felt in a while. I had finally told my mother about the person I was seeing. No judgments! She even approved of you! She also kept asking me to send you pictures of our family's Christmas, which was interesting to hear since I had never seen her so excited about my love life.

You and I also talked so much during my trip that we would send each other the word "over." It became our signal after a long paragraph. That way, the other person would know that it was safe for them to respond without interrupting the other person. We would also make puns out of it, saying random things like "we are OVER," which looking back at it now . . . I don't think it aged well.

However, the happy memories haven't been tarnished. They will remain happy as long as I hold them close to my heart.

We exchanged so many pictures of our Christmases, on different sides of the Atlantic, that it almost felt like we were spending it with one another. We even FaceTimed for hours, watching TV shows together, which resulted in my mother asking too many questions. Seeing her son acting like a teenager, with long phone calls and endless laughs, was weird to her, but it was all so special to me.

On the plane ride back, I was listening to music to kill some time. Since I was bored, I paid attention to one of the songs playing: "Until I Found You" by Stephen Sanchez. I wasn't that familiar with him, and at first, I was confused by his music. I thought it was peculiar how he introduced the song by talking about wanting to be wrapped in Georgia. It took me a while to realize that Georgia was actually a person and that he wasn't singing so passionately about a state. Then it hit me. He started singing about how she saved him from darkness and not wanting to fall in love again until he met her. All it took was for him to find her.

After my previous relationship hurt me, I wondered if I would ever find someone who would ignite the flame that was once in me. Substance abuse shattered all the dreams of that relationship. Everything we had been building together was destroyed, and it caused a big blow to my trust issues and my ability to love. Somehow, with you, I was as free as I could be. That flame was once again burning as bright as it could. Finding you was the proof that I could love again.

On the way back to New York, I had planned a layover in Canada to save some money. Little did I know that there would be a big snowstorm that ended up canceling countless flights. Including mine. I felt confident I wouldn't have a problem since I was going to land a few days after the storm. But I was wrong. The problem was that, because so many people were trapped in Canada without return flights, there weren't enough flights to take them home. The lack of crew members caused an additional hurdle for the airlines. At least that was the excuse they used to cancel mine. I was stuck in Canada! When I said my life felt like a movie, I should have specified it better. The airline leaving me at the airport made me realize my life was actually Portugal's favorite Christmas movie: *Home Alone*.

I didn't know when I was coming back since the airline couldn't book me a flight back home in the foreseeable future. All of them were completely booked as everyone was trying to leave as fast as possible. That was when I started to imagine myself spending New Year's Eve alone in Canada, and I didn't want it to become a reality. After I spent some long hours scrambling for a solution, I managed to get on a plane to Philadelphia the same day. Once I landed there, I planned to take a bus to New York City, not the ideal solution, but it was a solution. It was either that or waiting at the airport for an undetermined number of days.

The excitement about going back home rushed through my veins as I prepared my new itinerary. To be safe, I had booked the last bus of the day, but time would also be my enemy. My flight landed in Philadelphia much later than intended. Plus, they had lost my bag, which led me to file a lengthy lost luggage claim. I lost so many precious hours that I was out of breath when I got to the bus terminal with only two minutes to spare.

All I can say is that the layover turned out to be exhausting. Even though I arrived much later than anticipated, without a bag, and with a significant amount of stress on top of me, I was still grateful. I was going back home the same day as intended. You, being as sweet as always, asked me if there was anything you could do for me.

"In all honesty, just a hug," was my response to you. All I needed at that moment was just that. A hug. Something to make me feel content and relaxed again since all I desired was to see you again. Two weeks away from you had been too long. You invited me to your place once I arrived because you wanted to cheer me up. Although you knew I would only get there very late at night, long past your bedtime, you still wanted to make me happy.

Once I got to see you, I felt that. Happiness. I was finally reunited with you, ready to fall asleep in your arms. That moment to me was my own little piece of what heaven would be like. It was all I ever wanted; to feel safe in your arms and to decompress from all the stress I carried. Looking into your eyes and seeing your smile was the most genuine form of pleasure I had experienced. In that smile, I saw endless days of happiness. Endless days of coming home to the most beautiful thing I had ever seen. Endless new possibilities for me to fall for you even more. Over and over again.

One thing that took me by surprise was the fact that you were playing music in your living room when I got to your apartment. Coincidentally, the song that filled your apartment while I was being reunited with you was also "Until I Found You."

It was like something out of a movie, and time froze for the third time. At that moment, I realized destiny had brought us together, and it was marking its presence through that song. We found each other.

Today, I listened to the song again and relived that day. Although I was trying my best to avoid thinking about you, this memory was still able to shine through the cracks. There is no price I can pay to relive that moment or to feel your presence once again. Nothing will ever take me back to that night.

Then, for the first time, I took off my blinders. I only recalled one part of the lyrics I listened to on the plane, as it resonated with me. Today, I paid attention to the rest of the song. He finished his second verse by singing about how he would be there for his lover no matter what. He would never let her go again.

As clear as the day I was sitting on that plane, I realized that this song was indeed ours. I started juggling all my thoughts and emotions. Was this destiny once again? Telling me to keep fighting for you?

My ambition said yes. My desires said it wasn't over yet. My determination said there was still hope. My craving said that your lips would soon be reunited with mine. I just had to win you back.

I hope faith helps me in this journey because I'm on a quest for the most desirable thing in this world: happiness. Happiness with you. Happiness in the future I could share with you.

*Hey, can you lie to me and tell me the woman I spoke with today was your mom?*

I had this birthday brunch in New Jersey today that forced me to take a train from New York to your home state. The transportation system inside of New York City is entirely different than the one that connects the two states and, more often than not, I end up lost and confused, never knowing where I need to go to hop on the right train.

This time, while I was on a track trying to understand which direction the train was going, this older woman approached me. She was talking on the phone, and as soon as she noticed me, the only other person on the platform, she quickly started walking in my direction. I could hear her telling the person on the other end of the phone call that she had found someone to help her. Just like me, she was also lost.

After working together and finding out we were on the wrong train platform, we walked toward some plaques. While hoping they would lead us to the correct track, we started chatting to make the interaction less unpleasant and a little bit more personal.

She was a short older woman with blonde hair, kept together with a tie-dyed headband that complemented her partial hippie vibe. Most importantly, she had this sweet, welcoming, motherly aura that made me wish she was your mom.

I had never met your mom, and I didn't know what she looked like in person, but nothing could tell me it wasn't her. This woman was going to New Jersey, where your mom lives, after seeing one of her kids in New York. Not only that, but she was also on her way to see her other child in New Jersey. This matched where you and your brother lived. The odds were slim, but there was the possibility that it could be her!

That's when I started daydreaming. What if I were stuck inside an actual Hallmark movie scene? One where I was destined to meet your mom in the most random location ever possible. That one place you never go to, but the day you do, you run into all sorts of different people from your past. In that wild fantasy, she would fall in love with me after our conversation. Realizing that the man I so adored was her child, I would then have that motherly approval that the child in me was so desperately craving, and she would even put in a good word to her son for me. If those things happened in movies, why could they not happen in real life as well?

This encounter brought me back to our brunch date, where we saw some drag queens perform. While we were enjoying our meal and each other's company, out of the blue, she sent you a video of herself at a drag brunch as well. I remember being in ecstasy with the concept of having such a cool, supportive mom, someone who was so bored at home that she decided to grab her friends and go to a drag brunch.

I never had that type of support growing up, and even though a relationship with my parents is still being built, I don't think it will ever get to that point. I wondered how it must have felt to have that form of love from a mom while growing up. A thought that made me a bit jealous. I wanted to have experienced it as well.

I had always fantasized about meeting this supportive mom—your mom—but I never told you that. I was wrapped in this mystery she represented to me, but it would have sounded too crazy if I had verbalized it. If saying that would have made me sound crazy at the time, I think I would still be able to top that one. If I had ever gotten the chance to meet her and if she asked me what my intentions with her son were, I had an answer already prepared. I really wanted to impress her. It also doesn't help that I usually ask myself what my answer would be if a parent or a close friend of the person I am dating asked me one of those hard questions. The reality is that I would probably have said something simple. All I wanted was to make sure you brushed your teeth before going to bed.

I still think about her. She always represented an unmet need: to have someone who truly supports you and with whom you appreciate spending time. Moms are supposed to be there to love you, not to judge or shame you. Somehow, I felt that type of motherly love from this stranger as she asked me questions about my upbringing.

Eventually, we were sitting side by side on the train to New Jersey since we were both going in the same direction.

At some point, the question about my love life came up and I corrected her. There was no girlfriend; I was interested in men. I'm gay. That moment could have made or broken the perfect illusion I was drawing in my head. Worse, if she disliked gay people and decided to shame me, I would be in for a very uncomfortable train ride.

What happened next was unforeseeable and magical in its own way. Right after I told her about my sexuality, she told me the story of her own life, her struggles, and her upbringing. She had been a nurse during the HIV pandemic. It was remarkable to meet someone who faced hate because she loved the ones who weren't supposed to be loved by society back then. She told me incredible stories, and sad ones, too. In one of them, she explained how some of her friends told her that she wasn't allowed in their house at that time as no one knew what HIV was or how it was transmitted. She also told me a different powerful story. In this one, she was unable to keep her gloves on when she touched the face of someone who was about to pass away, despite the lack of knowledge about the so-called "gay disease." It would have been inhumane to deny someone that human touch before they passed away.

That made me wish I could still be there for you, to give you another hug after a hard day at work. Another gentle caress along your face while you're falling asleep on my chest. Another goodbye kiss. This is what I wanted to happen every single day, forever, until one day when one of these actions will be our last because age has worn us out. That was all I ever wanted.

Unfortunately, the two of us ended up like me and that stranger when we reached my destination. We said goodbye, thanked each other for the company on the train ride, and wished each other a nice day. Knowing that we would never see one another again.

I wish I was wrong, but my chest is heavy. As the doors closed, I realized I wouldn't have time to unpack any of my feelings. How I still crave my mother's approval as I never had it growing up, and it is something we are still working on. All I knew was that I had to rush and put on a fake smile to meet my friend at her birthday brunch. Pretending everything was fine while deep down I kept wishing that I had met your mom on that train platform so she could reconnect us.

Delusion is a person's best friend.

*Hey, today I finally brewed coffee again.*

After you left my life, I haven't been brewing that "sweet coffee" you fancied so much. The one you thought was perfect. Before, I used to drink at least two cups every single day, no matter how much sleep I had the night before. But I haven't been craving my morning cup for endless days.

I'm not sure if your departure just shocked my life in such a way that you unbalanced my metabolism, but the fact is it doesn't desire it anymore. Maybe I sleep better because I feel less anxious, not thinking about when I will get a text from you or when the next one will come since you didn't send me a good morning text.

I also have one more theory. Maybe my body is rejecting it because it reminds me of you.

I usually pour a mug and leave it by the end table next to my couch, letting it cool down while I do other things. Once I get back to it, every so often it's already lukewarm. When it gets to that point, I usually rush to reheat it since I'm always cold and I like to feel it warming me up.

I don't want to think about this scenario happening again, as it's another thing that reminds me of you. It's something else telling me you are gone. I don't want that bitter taste of room-temperature coffee to linger in my mouth and I don't want to associate that unpleasant taste with you.

I want to associate it with your face of excitement when I started brewing it and with that smile you had coming out of my bedroom. Ready to start a new day with me and a cup of coffee. I only want to connect you with pleasant situations like the thought of your lips kissing my forehead, making me feel safe. Wrapped in your arms under a fortress of blankets. That sweet kiss of death, of complete defeat. The one that would make me feel so powerless, unable to move, similar to someone putting a binder on a cat's neck. That was me, completely yours, wrapped in your essence.

All these feelings come to my mind as soon as I brew coffee and start smelling its comforting aroma. Taking a sip of it when it's lukewarm would be the equivalent of having all that disappear from my memory as my taste buds repel the taste.

You see, there is one interesting question I like to ask: *How do you like your coffee?* It's funny how everyone has a strong and robust preference, even if that choice is in the form of not liking it. Theoretically, we can say that for everything, but somehow this drink has one of the strongest followings. People take very stern stances on a preference and barely deviate from it. Drip, drip with some milk, espresso, pour-over, latte, cold brew . . . no coffee.

Somehow, you surprised me with your choice. As someone who has worked at a coffee shop before, I thought I had seen it all—from the common to the unusual, like with butter. But your choice was the wildest one, something I had never heard or thought about before. It was so crazy to me. I would have never guessed that, to avoid burning your tongue, you preferred it lukewarm. You were an impatient person, and sometimes you would forget to let it cool down. By using this technique, your tongue would always be safe.

How quirky! Hearing this explanation was so charming and captivating. It truly was something unique that reinforced the magical entity that you were. You were always able to find a way to surprise me.

With that in mind, I would get out of bed before you even woke up to start preparing our morning fuel. I would then pour half of it into a cup, allowing it to cool down before I headed back to bed to lay next to you for a few more minutes. You would then provide me with morning kisses in return for the lukewarm coffee I was about to give you. Only later would I pour my cup. I wanted to feel its warmth throughout my body.

I think coffee is such a peculiar way to show affection for someone, whether they need the caffeine to wake up or whether they're addicted to this drink. One way or the other, it's an interesting dynamic to pay attention to. By brewing it for the other person to savor when they wake up, you end up marking a ritual for the beginning of their day. Even if they leave right after, that caffeine rush will stay with them for a while. They will carry a piece of your love with them.

Today, I felt the need to brew it once again, although I was afraid of all the memories it would awaken in me. As I took a sip of that hot drink, I realized it didn't taste the same as it once did. My body is still rejecting the thought of that ritual we once had. Without you, life isn't the same. The clear indicator is that I can't even find pleasure in something I was once so addicted to.

I hope this book works its magic because I miss you. I miss our mornings on the couch, watching TV. I miss that feeling of enjoying my warm cup of coffee while you stood by my side, happily sipping yours lukewarm. I miss that kiss on my forehead I would get when I went back to bed while your coffee cooled down. I miss that smile when you realized I was back to cuddle some more before it was time to start another beautiful day.

I miss *you*.

# Step Two:

# Anger

Day Nine

*Hey, I hooked up with someone today. You have got to be kidding me. How could it be that awful?*

I don't understand when people say you should get intimate with someone to forget a past lover. It doesn't work for me. Getting together with a random person for one night, the typical rebound, will never ease the pain. The reality is that I shouldn't have to force myself to be busy all the time to avoid thinking about you, and I definitely didn't need to use a body next to mine to avoid missing yours.

Today, I made the mistake of thinking that a random person would make me forget about you. Even if only for a moment. As soon as I walked through the door to his apartment, I immediately started judging the situation.

I tried to assess what the apartment looked like, hoping to find comfort in it and wanting to return to that place. If that hookup had a cozy space, maybe I would end up staying there for a long time, and everything would be fine. I would have found a new home I felt comfortable in. A replacement for you.

An apartment is a gateway to get to know someone, from how many pillows they have to the art on the wall. Or the lack of it. So much can be said by looking at how someone has decorated the space they go back to every day. The place where they should feel the most comfortable. I do miss yours, and I was trying to find a strange sense of comfort in a stranger's living room because being fond of it would be the first step to moving on. Or so I thought.

I met this person on one of those so-called dating apps, and before I entered his apartment, I wondered if my life would change. If this hookup was passionate and perfect, I could move on as quickly as I fell in love with you.

I took a deep breath before opening the door, which I was putting so much hope into. After scanning his studio, I realized that it resembled a hotel more than a home. There was no personality. There wasn't a single trinket in sight from a past trip, a gift from a friend, or a personalized object that hinted at his personality. It was a boring room with some cheap chairs next to the countertop, a generic TV stand, and a bed. There was nothing else, not even something as simple as a rug. But at least the bed was on a bedframe!

I stopped to think. Why did I think this was a good idea? This encounter would clearly lead me to block him afterward. The place was so uninviting that it made me not want to go back there. It's not a shocker, but I didn't find my forever home that day.

The worst part happened when he started kissing me. I know I'm desperate and lonely, but I was able to find someone who would beat me in my own game. He probably has been playing it for longer than I have. I could feel it. I could feel his desperation with every kiss, making me feel uncomfortable. I was fearful I would eventually become this person. Loneliness sure is a quick journey to desperation. The thought of it slowly awakened a fury in me I didn't know I had. I feared being that person in the future, but I also resented you for not being there to satisfy these primordial needs.

All I wanted to do was to close my eyes and think of you. Picturing you next to me, I tried my best to transport the image of you into that stranger's bed. But there was not a slight similarity in sight that I could hold on to. Not a smell. Not a touch. Not a kiss. Nothing. Although I tried my best to imagine it was you, there was nothing I could do. There was not an ounce of physical similarity. Every kiss was a realization of this. I hated the way his tongue would meet my lips. It gave me chills. Whenever we touched or hugged, I felt cold and empty inside.

I don't know if the hookup was a mistake, as I was clearly trying to use it to avoid my feelings, or if it was simply the other person's fault paired with our lack of chemistry. All I knew was that I had to leave as fast as possible. Every touch made me miss yours even more. It made me wonder if I would ever find someone whose lips I could compare to yours. Thinking that a random person would make me feel better is a lie, a big old sack of crap.

This man wasn't you, and he could never be you. Why did I even think that a random hookup would solve all my sadness in the first place? Why am I this stupid? He didn't have your touch or our chemistry.

He also didn't have our shared history; he and I were strangers. It wasn't like the two of us, where we already knew what each other liked and how to please one another. We already had the classic conversation about what the other person is into. Even though you didn't know the answer to that at first—you hadn't stopped to think about yourself that deeply—I didn't see you differently. It could have been the first red flag, someone who doesn't know themselves. Someone so busy that they never stop to think about their needs and wants. Or maybe not. I wanted to believe that it wasn't that bad. You just had to figure yourself out a little bit better and stop hiding in that protective shell you call work.

My body didn't connect for that long with that casual body. I rushed out after giving an excuse since I wasn't feeling comfortable or getting any pleasure. That sensual dance without you was meaningless. All I wanted was to leave through that door and be thrown back into the real world and leave this make-believe realm that my fantasy was creating. I would rather face the cold truth, no matter how much I hate it, than to deny it with lies.

When I left, I still couldn't stop thinking about you and our little things and games in the bedroom. Like that playlist I played so my roommate wouldn't hear anything. That same one that shocked you when you heard me tell my home assistant device to play it for the first time. You looked me in the eyes and asked me, "Cum Jams?" with the most puzzled expression, only to have me correct you. You misheard me. The correct name was actually "Calm Jams." You then learned the right name of the playlist, and I learned the specific places where you liked to be touched.

It was all so magical between us. We even came up with that stupid little code for when we were apart and were feeling sexually aroused. We had this emoji we would send back and forth whenever our minds were saying something our hands didn't dare to text. "You're so freaking hot, and all I want right now is to have you in my bed with me." That's what that emoji meant, a booty call of some sort. It was our special secret. Our inside joke. One emoji that would say that there was no one else in this world we would rather be kissing. No one else we would rather wrap in a tight hug and call ours.

I miss that. And I'm upset that it's over. Like that other game we had, it's *over*. OVER.

*Hey, I finally got the courage to take your stupid toothbrush out of my bathroom today.*

It had been standing there in the cup holder for so long, in the hopes that one day I would see you use it once again. Who knew something so small could be so magnetic? The sight of it reminded me of the nights you spent at my apartment, usually on the weekend. And geez . . . those periods from Saturday until Sunday afternoon were my favorite part of the week because I got to spend them with you. I even felt the need to give a cute nickname to those hours I cherished so deeply. I used to call these periods by your name, followed by the word "time."

I would wait impatiently for that time of the week, like a child waiting to open their presents on Christmas. Those hours I waited, full of anticipation, would help me get through the week. Nowadays, I sometimes forget which day of the week it is. I don't care either way because I'm not looking forward to anything in particular. It's just a Thursday, a normal Thursday. When before, it meant that, in two nights, I would get to hang out with you. I would finally get the opportunity to spend some time with you before going home to spend the rest of the night with you in my arms.

Getting home was also a signal for another mindless ritual. I would announce that I was going to brush my teeth before going to bed, and you would follow my lead every single time. You joked about needing someone to hold you accountable for brushing yours. Somehow your behavior reminded me of my dad, maybe for the worst, but there were still some similarities. Was it comfort around you, or was I following old habits and patterns?

Interestingly, I don't know, because I never brushed my teeth shirtless (your favorite type of pajama) next to my dad. He and I never laughed as we shared a look while our beards got covered in toothpaste. I also never made jokes to him, asking if he was going to swallow the toothpaste like I did to you. You loved mint chocolate chip ice cream, and to me, they had the same taste. What an abomination of a flavor . . .

Who knew a toothbrush could hold so many memories? A simple blue toothbrush. Impatiently, day after day, it stood there waiting for you, hoping to see you again. Like I wait for another kiss.

It also reminds me of when you would shower at my apartment, the only place I would shower with you. I'm very particular about sharing this experience, and the main reason is that (you guessed it) I'm always cold. My apartment has this rainforest shower that would sit on top of us. With a step backward, one of us would be warm again, without having to awkwardly spin while holding the other person's body so no one slips. We could both coexist in that tub. We didn't have to tap dance around each other to get to the water to avoid freezing to death. I love how those moments were so silly but so endearing, especially as we were so close to each other.

One of the times we showered together was when I noticed the lead fillings in your teeth. At first, I thought something was stuck there, but you joked about it and assured me that it wasn't. You started telling me the story of how everyone thought you were much older than you really were, all thanks to some archaic dental work you received in the town you grew up in. Those practices were outdated, but somehow you still got them. I guess that's why you had joked about wanting someone to make sure you brushed your teeth, the reason why I thought your mom would like that influence in your life. Someone who helped keep you on top of your dental hygiene.

If you had already reminded me of my dad, the lead in your teeth, in turn, made me think about my mother's smile. She had those fillings as well. It's impressive how something as simple as brushing my teeth can bring back so many memories. It takes me back to my parents and my childhood, and at the same time, it also brings me back to you.

All those memories were unlocked by a single, almost new toothbrush. That's why I had to get rid of it. Those thoughts bring me so much sadness because I won't relive them again. I hate that object for making me relive them every single day when I see it next to mine.

It's also fascinating to see how the bristle from yours was barely used; it hadn't struggled like mine. It makes sense because you only came to my apartment once or twice a week, but it's still curious how, by contrast, mine was damaged, beaten, and in need of a replacement. It had been put to work so many times, and somehow it was still standing there strong and ready to fight again. Yours sat there new, pristine, and sharp. A toothbrush that hadn't seen the worst and hadn't been put to the test. *Just like you.* When a difficulty appeared in our relationship, you quit instead of trying to fight for us. You went on to find a new one instead of brushing our difficulties, trying to improve what could be such a thrilling future.

Instead of finishing things without *what ifs*, knowing that we tried our best, but it just didn't work out, I'm left full of resentment. You threw away something I treasured so deeply. There is a word that I can associate with my feelings: *pain.* I'm mad that you gave up and moved on so easily, as if it all meant nothing. I'm mad you chose to walk away instead of growing stronger together. I'm mad you didn't even try. Because of that, your toothbrush can no longer live in my cup holder, in my memory, or with me.

Even though I threw it away full of resentment, I do hope you're still brushing your teeth. Although I'm furious at you, inside of me there is a part that still wants to see you smile again.

*Hey, today I finally got the courage to delete your presence from my phone.*

Lately, part of me has been feeling helpless, craving a re-connection with you, while the other half of me constantly tells me I'm being an idiot. Facing the truth hurts. And so does shattering the delusion that I'll get to see you again. It stresses me out. I'm unable to sit still. It's a slowly creeping feeling that takes over my veins, making me feel uneasy within my own skin. It makes me wish I could shed my exterior like a snake.

Usually, these feelings come up when I see your face on my phone. It's always hard whenever I press the share button and see your picture in my contacts. I hate how it makes me feel, pissed at myself for allowing someone to make me feel worthless. My stomach would turn into a knot imagining the happiness I once felt whenever I saw your selfie next to your morning text. It was one of those knots so strong that it would cause me to throw up any food in me.

That's why today I grabbed my phone and finally deleted your contact photo—and the emoji I had next to your name. That was the doing of the part of me that calls me an idiot for still caring so much. The one that's furious at myself for being this way.

The other half, the helpless one, didn't want to take the next step and delete your number. Hope is still there, that little spark to the fuel that is reconnecting in the future.

Up to this day, I felt like it was so magical how my contact photo of you was a selfie you sent me after a long day at work. You had worked an overnight shift and were exhausted, ready to fall asleep. While looking miserable, you still gathered the courage to mimic sending me a good morning kiss while doing a peace sign with your fingers. Words can't begin to describe how adorable you looked. In all honesty, in my eyes, you looked tremendously attractive, no matter how unenergized you appeared to be.

It's special how I would find you good-looking, even in the most unattractive situations. I say that fully knowing that, luckily, I never saw you puke (that would probably ruin that fantasy in my head).

Nevertheless, I would still find you attractive day after day, no matter the situation. Even if I was waking up in the morning next to you, with sleep crust all over your eyes and a path of dried drool from your lips to the pillow, I still found you charming. I was at peace. I felt like it was home.

Today, seeing your face was starting to become too much. I decided I could no longer see that photo anymore. It was all too real, and I had to push you away from my brain. We might share similar views because you also muted me on Instagram after I uploaded some photos from a wedding I had attended. I noticed, after that day, you stopped seeing my stories. Was it also hard on you to see me smile? I hope it was. I hope you regret your decision. I hope that seeing me happy made your blood boil. I hope that seeing me smile also made you uncomfortable with yourself.

I doubt you're in as much pain as I am, given that it was so easy for you to walk away, but I want you at least to feel part of the pain I feel. And part of the frustration as well. I'm irritated that I screwed up and I will never find someone like you again. Staying in the relationship and resolving our issues would have been a simple solution. Our differences weren't that big of a deal. Instead, you would rather be lonely than be vulnerable and ruin your "knight in shining armor" fantasy. You still prefer to believe that someday someone will come in and be your total match, without an argument, ever. For you, having a roadblock was a chip in that armor. You realized that things weren't perfect and that I could possibly not be *the one* as it would require some work ironing out our differences to grow together. You still think that one day the right person will come, and everything will fall together perfectly, forever. Well, you are wrong, and I feel bitter about the way you think.

That view alone made you reject all the positive things we had, making you focus on the negative ones instead. You wanted an excuse to leave. Running away to avoid having another person break your heart. You had to protect yourself because our conflict was a sign that we were not meant to be together. It would inevitably lead you to a broken heart. Or so you thought.

A relationship requires work; it's about growing together. How couldn't you see that? I'm mad that you revealed your avoidant attachment style and decided to run away from everything we were building together.

The other thing I had to delete from my phone was the little emoji next to your name. It made you stand out, among all my contacts, a little too much.

I have this habit of saving a person's first name next to an emoji. This character represents who they are and helps me differentiate between two people with the same name and also gives me a visual representation of who they are. Sometimes, I won't save a phone number if I don't know which emoji to use. I need to know what makes that person special, what's their quirk. I don't want to choose a simple emoji related to their job. I want to select an emoji that reflects their personality or a memory we share.

For yours, I didn't have to think too hard about it. I knew exactly which one would be the clear winner in the sea of emojis: a Christmas tree. Just like that, I had your name followed by a tall, colorful green pine surrounded by lights. It does sound like a Hallmark cliché, but I can't deny the fact that you love Christmas. You were so involved in it that you were able to make me want to celebrate the holiday again. I was starting to get frustrated with the constant long travels to see my family, with how I associated it with me going back into the closet for the extended family, and with all the money spent on so many gifts. Yet, through it all, on the first date, you made me care about Christmas again.

I saw the spark in your eyes and the excitement in your voice when you talked about the upcoming carols. You were looking forward to seeing every place transform into a blinking festival of lights and the peace and happiness that the season brings. You even taught me about the importance of having a backup gift. Something simple that you can give to someone in case they end up giving you a present unexpectedly. You were so excited that, for a second, I wondered if Christmas had become a pyramid scheme and you were trying to recruit another elf.

I was wrong. You just loved Christmas in a way I wished you had loved me back.

Because of all that, I will always think of you when Christmas comes. When the wind gets colder. When my sheets feel empty. When I miss the feeling of you warming up my bed next to me.

Today, I used that resentment, the frustration of losing you, as strength to knock down the tree next to your name. With each swing I took, I remembered it wasn't Christmas anymore and that I must tear you down from my life because you hurt me so much.

*Hey, I can't believe it's snowing outside.*

It has been so long since it last snowed. In fact, I haven't seen the weather like this in a long time, and it makes me sad. The truth is that the white powdery look on top of the buildings is enough to shatter my heart into pieces. I love snow, and I know you love it, too. I mean . . . it wouldn't be a white Christmas without it, right?

I picture you looking through your window with the most beautiful smile possible, marveling at the snow coming down. While on the other side of town, I see the same sky. But I also see my reflection through the window, and I can see my broken heart.

I regret not being able to kiss you on a snowy day when we were together. I wanted to see the snowflakes cover your face. Marvel at your black beard turning white, then pulling you closer to feel the cold weather disappear with the warmth our kisses would provide. I wanted to give you that foolish romantic experience since we never had the chance to see snow together.

I would have liked to pull my hammock back up on my balcony so that I could lay on it with you. This way, we could have gazed at the snowfall while we shared the most profound hug, turning ourselves into the other person's human blanket.

Do you still remember that hammock? You once had told me you missed being in one, and by coincidence, I had one on my balcony. The problem, at the time, was that the hot weather had ended, and I didn't want the coming rainy season to damage it. It was time to retire it until the warm months came back. However, there was still one way we could have one last hoorah with it.

One night, when you slept at my place, I pulled it out of my balcony into the living room. My roommate was out of town, so we could take as much space as we wanted. We then spent a whole day watching movies lying on it. I felt like a true teenager all over again. We laughed so much and so hard that my stomach hurt. It felt like a coming-of-age movie where time stands still at the end. Right before the most emblematic words come, the words that transform those teenagers into adults. In our case, it solidified how we were meant to be together.

Do you remember that? It looked so out of this world that I sent a photo of it to my friends. The ones who pushed us to go on a date. All of them made fun of the fact that, as soon as my roommate was out of town, I turned my apartment into a Club Med. They weren't wrong, especially since I had cooked you a true continental breakfast of three different dishes that morning. I miss that, and I hope you do, too.

It was still early in our story, but I miss that feeling. That feeling when you know things will work out. When both people can coexist so perfectly together while enjoying each other's company and laughing nonstop.

Damn . . . how I miss seeing you laugh. Do you know it still haunts me in my dreams? Yes, I still dream of you every night. I wake up missing you next to me every morning. Asking myself why I can only have you visit me in my thoughts at night but not in the morning. Instead of you, I only have a cold blanket to wrap around myself, so I can watch the snow fall and pave the floor white.

The weirdest aspect of it all is that, although I know how much you would have loved to see this snowy night, there is a part inside of me that doesn't want you to see it. I'm still so angry at you. So angry you dropped such a magical thing at the sight of the first conflict. So angry you didn't try. So angry at you for hurting me. So angry that you threw it all away. I'm so angry that I hope you don't get to experience this memory that would have been so dear to us.

Since it isn't below freezing outside, what once were snowflakes are now slowly being converted into raindrops. I hope it continues like that. I know you're at work now, and I hope that once you leave, the rain has washed it all away.

I don't want you to leave work and feel happy with the memory that we should have shared. I should be the one kissing and cuddling you while we watch this symbolic classic Christmas experience. Call me selfish all you want, but since you took that dream from me, I hope you never see how much it snowed tonight.

Because of that, I also want to take away that happiness from you. This should have been our moment! It could have been our moment if you had fought for us just a little bit. This would have been another unforgettable memory with you, one that I would cherish forever. Unfortunately, I'm sitting on my couch, wrapped in melancholy, wrapped in my blanket, wrapped in sorrow, wrapped in a level of anger I haven't experienced in a long time.

No matter how often I wish you were here or in an imaginary place we would call home, with a hammock in the middle of the living room we could use to watch Hallmark movies, I'm still angry with you. I wish we had that place where we could build a foundation for so many more positive memories because, with you, I was the happiest. But at the end of the day, the reality is that I won't live those desires with you.

Just like a kid who found the most delicious lollipop before dropping it to the ground, I'm annoyed. I'm annoyed at myself for not holding you tighter so you wouldn't slip away from my fingers. I'm annoyed at those *what ifs* that will forever haunt me. I'm annoyed at you for letting go as soon as the first obstacle came.

*Hey, I'm curious. Where do you want to be five years from now?*

This question usually has people scrambling to find an answer in the professional world. Do I want to be a manager at my company? Do I want to have graduated from a specific program? Do I want to stay at my job? Do I want to move to a new city? Do I want to publish a book?

To me, this concept is different. My *where* is more of a place, a feeling, and a moment. A moment that I want to share with you. I had hoped that five years from now, we could have had the chance to build a safe space. Somewhere you would feel comfortable coming home to after a long day at work. A place where I would know that, regardless of what you wanted, you would know where to go. It could be a space to unwind, have a laugh, or simply a silent hug, but I would be there for you. A balanced dynamic that can only happen if two people really know one another well and trust and respect each other.

Sounds simple, right? Then why was it so hard for us to get there?

If you always said you loved how much I respected your space and how understanding I was of your busy schedule, why was it so hard to tell me that you were burned out with work? I would have loved to know it was the reason why texting had been a hard task for you toward the end. It was starting to become difficult for you to find the strength to catch up with my texts when, after work, all you wanted was to dissociate from the real world. I would have understood the situation.

Instead, I tried doing more and more because I saw you slip away from my fingertips. I didn't realize the pressure was freaking you out, and because of that, I tried holding onto you tighter, which led you to feel suffocated. Why couldn't we have communicated these feelings back then? Why didn't you tell me your needs?

It sounds like a problem with such a simple solution, or were you afraid of ruining such a quasi-perfect thing by introducing conflict? The thought that, somehow, we weren't the perfect match after all? Were you fearful of ruining the textbook image of a fairy tale? Would I no longer be *the one*, the knight in shining armor if there was a minor conflict? For me to be your *the one*, was I supposed to come already programmed to understand your every move, without questions? Was I expected to sail smoothly through the daggers you were throwing at me? Or were you just a coward? Who ran away with your tail behind your legs . . .

I thought that *the one* was that person who creates a safe space for you to share everything because you know they won't judge you. Instead, they will work on overcoming the obstacles. That's love. Not bottling up your feelings and thoughts, which is such a dangerous thing to do. You will end up with only one possible outcome: exploding. Suddenly, you will believe that the relationship was doomed to fail because there are broken pieces everywhere!

Sometimes the issues can be hard and detrimental, like having the other person constantly disrespecting and hurting you. In these cases, no matter how much two people talk and try to fix it, there is rarely a way to repair things. Other issues like alcoholism or racism are no joke. But understanding a busy schedule and being burned out with work? Understanding that I was doing too much to bring you closer and that I should slow down because I was stressing you out even more because you weren't able to match me? Is that the worst problem you can come up with? The deal breaker in a relationship? Screw you.

I understand that we were the anxious attachment style meeting the avoidant one. I can see how I was desperate for validation that you loved me. I can also see how I was constantly trying to find it in your actions. Meanwhile, you were terrified that having a partner would mean disrupting the independent lifestyle you had going on for yourself.

I also know that I'm not perfect. I'm deeply flawed, too. I'm simply a person trying to navigate my insecurities and problems. Just like you. The biggest difference is that I understand no one will ever be fully ready for love. No one will ever be perfect enough to be ready to date. It's all about how we find someone who embraces us, someone who will hold our hand while both of us navigate the many obstacles of life.

We will keep growing in our lifetime, finding new ways to improve ourselves. Two people in a relationship will be different, year after year, as they mature. But they do so to-gether. They understand their partner will allow them to grow and will challenge them to do better as *we are never fully ready*. I see the growth I could do with you because I need to investi-gate my own actions. I need to realize that I also need to heal my desperation for love. I'm deeply flawed.

I hope one day you will understand that there is no Prince Charming. No one will click with you perfectly and have all the same lifestyle choices and interests as you. That's loving *yourself*. Loving someone else is fighting for what they both believe in. It's believing in a future where we could watch a movie after a busy day at work, with your head on my shoulder as you doze off to sleep, your drool wetting my T-shirt . . . That's love to me.

To me, five years from now is a home built on respect and trust.

# Step Three:

# Bargaining

Day Fifteen

*Hey, today I played a board game as your favorite animal.*

I know you weren't the biggest fan of board games when we were dating, but I sincerely want to thank you for trying to play one with me that one time. Back then, you knew how much I loved them, so you tried to give them a chance. In all honesty, that's what relationships are based on—trying your partner's interests. Even if you don't enjoy them, at least you can say that you tried. This way, you won't hold it against them for forcing you to try something you didn't like. Instead, you stepped out of your comfort zone, and you can say that you experimented with their hobbies because it would bring them happiness. That's why it meant a lot to me when you played a board game with me. I hope you know that.

It was so sweet to me how we played that game with our hands revealed so I could help you out. We were playing a game that resembled a battle Yahtzee, for lack of a better explanation. You were a gunslinger, and I was a samurai, battling one another by rolling dice and using special cards. It wasn't a cooperative game, but we still played it like it was one. I advised you on which cards to use against me, and I also went easy on you. I might have missed a few steps on purpose to give you a better shot at winning, no pun intended.

I tried to make you feel like we were neck and neck because I didn't want to discourage you from playing with me again. I wanted you to think you were a natural at it, even though your ADHD was already making you focus on something else. I told you how to do things, and in the end, I managed to bend the rules a little bit so we could tie. Although we knew it was your last turn before I won, I didn't want it to happen. I let you reroll the dice more times than you were allowed to and I kept telling you to redo it with a different strategy. Ultimately, we did manage to end the game in a tie, and your joy was priceless. No losers. No winners. Just two lovers caught in the crossfire of a samurai and a gunslinger.

Even though that was the only time we played a board game together, I'm happy because we did it at least once. It meant a lot to me. I was comfortable knowing that the one match we played didn't make you a fan of this hobby. *At least you tried.* As a result, I didn't take it personally since I'm not supposed to date a carbon copy of myself, someone who has all my interests. You gave it a shot, and I appreciated your commitment to try to expand your horizons.

At the end of the day, I had other groups of people to play games with. One of them loved this game where several factions, who live in a forest, are fighting for victory points. There are birds, cats, lizards, mice, otters, and even a raccoon named Vagabond. The first time I played it, I decided to go for the birds because they were one of the easiest factions. After that, I decided that I would like to play as the raccoon since each faction has different rules and mechanics, and I wanted to try a new one. Upon choosing this faction, I realized I wouldn't want to play with another one for a long time. The reason was you.

I had to decide which raccoon leader I would play, and one of them caught my eye among the list of options. If only you knew the excitement I experienced when I saw one of them was a possum! All I wanted was to run to you so I could show you this game, hoping it would convert you into a gamer.

After that match, I would only choose the possum every single time we played that game. It made me feel closer to you, as if we were back in my living room rolling dice and playing with cards. The best part is that I won every single time. No matter which strategy I chose, with you in spirit, we were unstoppable.

When you love someone, the weird things they do and care about don't scare you. You end up embracing them. Instead of looking at them as reasons to break up, you view them as reasons to think that your partner is special and different. It's the little things that make a heart. It was the collection of all your quirks that made you who you were. One of them was your deep passion for possums. How those memes with this animal would make you smile, or how you made me ask you out on Valentine's Day like a schoolgirl. I got you an empty book with a possum on the cover, followed by a paper that read:

*Do you want to be my Valentine?*

*[ ] Yes*

*[ ] Yes, but with a possum journal.*

I know you love to journal, so I hoped you would think of me more often when you used my gift. That you would put me on top of your lists, as you sometimes did with your weekly to-do list, no pun intended. As it happened often, the week would go by and you would notice that we hadn't seen each other, so you had to make amends. At that moment, I felt forgotten and sad, and when I told you how I felt, you realized that putting someone on a weekly to-do list wasn't the most romantic gesture. You were just so busy with work that it was all you could do.

I let my emotions get the best of me. I should have been a little bit more understanding of your needs. You should have better communicated your problems with me and what was bothering you. Neither of us is perfect, but is perfection necessary for a successful and healthy relationship? Shouldn't a relationship be about growing together in a safe space?

If you agree, we can extend this game of love for one more round. We can then manipulate the odds as we did once before when we played that game together. This time, we would get to the outcome we both wanted, like we did back then.

At the end of the day, don't worry, because whenever I see a possum, I will think of you. Not because I find you hideous and repulsive but because I know that it would have made you smile.

*Hey, since we can't do relationship health checks anymore can we do a mental one instead?*

I was recently at Barnes and Noble trying to find the most hopelessly romantic book they had. One of the cheesy ones. The type of novel that makes some people say, "Ew, *love*." I wanted a story about two guys in love, one that would bring me to tears and make me feel like I was living vicariously through their experiences. If I couldn't feel love, at least I could live it through someone else's lens.

While I was trying to find where this section was, I found the self-help one instead. Curiosity led me there, and I ended up leaving with two books under my arm that would hopefully change my way of looking at relationships. Neither of them was a romance. In fact, I didn't even make it to that section. I made myself believe that I should start reframing my way of viewing the world instead of constantly living in a fantasy land.

One of them was called *It's Not Me, It's You: Break the Blame Cycle*, which featured two therapists talking about the ups and downs of their relationship and how they improved themselves to love better. The second one was *Codependent No More*. I decided to start by reading the former. I told myself that it would be easier for me to start my healing journey by being able to blame both of us before diving into myself and only having myself to blame.

I gravitated to these two books because I have been reading about codependency and how I fit into its definition. That was when I realized that I had become my mother, a thought that scares me to my core. I noticed how I have been repeating her actions, the same ones that make me feel suffocated whenever I visit home.

That realization was crucial for me to see that there is still so much I need to work on myself. There is still unhealed trauma from past relationships and even from my childhood. I do need to complete myself and not let a partner be the missing piece in my life, or I will never find happiness.

If I'm unable to complete myself, what would happen if I lost my partner in an accident? A life-taking accident, so I don't blame myself for letting someone walk away from me. Would I be crying at the cemetery for the rest of my days, praying that one day I would be reunited with them in the afterlife? Is there even an afterlife? What if there is, but this partner has moved on and found another soulmate in this realm, and I'm left by myself crying because I have spent my living life waiting for someone who would never be mine again?

I need to break free from all these habits and thoughts. I need some independence! Hopefully not hyper-independence like you, but I need to find that sweet balance so I don't completely flip the script and become too closed off. All I know is that I must find myself and start to love myself first!

Having said all that . . . thank you! Thank you for making me cry for days and days and days in a row. It was what it took to make me see that I was a desperate ball of anxiety, waiting for love from someone else. I was waiting for *the one* to come to save me from my despair and angst.

I wonder what would have happened if you had never broken up with me. Would we have stayed together, and I would've turned into a stress machine, overthinking about why you were constantly pulling away from me? Would I be constantly sad because I didn't get a response from your text messages in a timely manner or a good morning text? Sad because we finally moved in together, intertwining our lives so much that I don't know what to do with myself since I'm no longer counting the days to see you? Sad because our kids left for college, leaving the home empty, and I have no purpose? Sad because I don't love myself?

At the same time, I don't have only myself to blame for this. It's important to learn how to trust and fight for what we believe in when facing adversities. At the end of the day, that isn't the type of behavior I need in my life. Someone who will abandon me when things get rough sounds like a recipe for disaster.

I can't shake the feeling that if you can't fight, if you can only run away, then there is the possibility that you will leave me when things get challenging. When we are deciding which house to buy. When we have our first child, and you can't sleep at night. That isn't a healthy way to live. You will never be able to envision a future with someone like that because your vision will be fogged with fear.

Detaching isn't an easy feat. I still love the idea of you. What you could symbolize in my life, what you could be, and what you could do to my life. I still love your *potential*. I want that; I want to fight for that! The issue is that I don't love this side of you. I could find excuses for your behavior and stretch them as far as love goes, but this crack would only grow wider and wider, so wide it would eventually tear us apart, leaving us both stranded.

I guess you still need to work on yourself as well, or maybe you weren't *the one* after all. Maybe. Or maybe you were. I still don't know if I deserve someone better or if maybe you were as good as I allowed you to be. I had to be more compassionate to myself for you to grow with me. All I know is that this is all talk and no action. I need to detach myself from this ideal fantasy I have of you and see the flaws for what they are.

I hope I'm doing my best to do so and avoid being overly optimistic and delusional. I still have this desire where you see these issues and decide to try to fight them next to me. While I fight my own. I believe in us, and I believe we can work it out together. These are my hopes and manifestations, as some people like to call it. I still don't know if I should name them delusions or dreams. It's hard to try to see the positive side through these murky waters, and I frequently wonder if I should even try. There is still codependency in me that, every so often, keeps telling me to fight this battle and that maybe it isn't all lost. We just had to see our issues to be able to solve them.

I hope our future shines as bright as how your smile made me feel. I hope that one day, down the line, after we both have grown, we get the chance to reconnect. I can see our future in vivid technicolor. I see it being made of a fort of all the pillows and blankets you have collected over the years. I see a future where we put on cardboard vests and wield swords and go fight the dragon together, the adversity of relationships. We'd be unfazed by how burnt our castle gets in the process because we both know that we can always rebuild it, but not if the dragon keeps running among us, casting flames of doubt into our future.

We can only live that childlike fantasy if we work together. If we both realize our problems and accept to fight them as one. I know that I'm ready to tackle my issues, but there is a question I don't know the answer to: *Are you ready to fight yours?* I know your past hasn't been so kind to you. You were forced to experience the worst, but that can't be an excuse anymore for you not wanting to be a better person, someone better for yourself, for me, and for us. I can't fight this war alone.

So please, open your eyes and stop living in this Hallmark fantasy. I want to fight for this relationship that I believe in so much. I don't want to keep tearing myself apart, trying to fight the thorns that surround the castle of your heart alone.

*Hey, was it also hard for you to tell your mom that we were no longer together?*

Today, I finally told my mother that we broke up, which was undoubtedly hard. I couldn't stop tearing up while we chatted on the phone. My words cut me like daggers coming out of my mouth. I was realizing that all my dreams and fantasies were no longer coming to fruition and that I had to destroy the imaginary future I had built for us in my head. This wasn't only hard for me but for my mother as well. It hurt her to see her child hurt. She is also codependent, and her mental well-being is dependent on mine.

That fact always pressured me when I was younger to not have any sign of weakness, or she would suffer, too. If I expressed a negative emotion, like sadness, it meant that she failed at being a mother. This codependency also makes her desperate for me to have children. Although I'm close to hitting thirty, I'm still not there yet, and she can't see that there is still time in my life. She is eager to have someone else to take care of because that makes her happy. She always needs to mother someone.

When I went home for Christmas, after meeting you, she showered me with questions about you. It was impressive since it was the first time I had ever told her anything about the guy I was seeing. She was so involved in the process that, although it did feel fantastic to be accepted at first, it also felt a bit off. She would make me take photos of our Christmas table or even of our Christmas tree to send to you. It felt like she was desperate. She so desperately wanted me to find someone stable so I could realize the fantasy she had built in her head. Her dream was for me to have a happy relationship and kids. A dream she now had to destroy as well as you are no longer in my life.

I will never forget how she asked me to tell her things about you. It isn't an easy question to answer! What will you tell your parents that isn't some cliché answer you could hear about anyone?

"He knows some Portuguese because he learned it in college."

"You already told me that," she said. It was strike number one. My mother wasn't impressed, and it was visible on her face.

"He is family-oriented."

"That's good," she said, while her eyebrows slowly traveled upward, demonstrating that she developed some interest in you.

"He loves Christmas."

"OHHHH, that's perfect." Damn it! Your love for Christmas was the easiest way to win her over.

She then asked me for a photo of you, and I decided to show her something that would showcase your personality even better. I showed her a video of you singing that

Christmas classic "Dominick the Donkey" at a bar, and she complimented you after watching it. It felt like that was finally it! At last, I had gotten my mother's stamp of approval!

Was this the validation I have been seeking since I was a child? To be supported by my parents after so many years of hiding my sexuality? To have them invite you over for next Christmas, as she did?

I wonder what she was expecting when she extended that invitation. Was her fantasy telling her that you would ask her for my baby photos, so she could make you dream about having children? I can't lie, I would have done the same if I had ever gone to your mom's house. I was dying to see what you looked like when you were a kid! I was curious to know if you were chubby and adorable, or skinny and clearly waiting for puberty to take effect for your beauty to blossom. I was crying in most of my baby photos, and I was intrigued to know what yours look like. I was curious about your past because while I could sketch our future, the past was already written. It was already living in some photo albums that I was dying to discover on a Christmas morning.

Today, I hope that, during that phone call, one of my biggest fears didn't materialize. I'm afraid of disappointing my parents.

Next time, I know not to be so quick to tell them about who I'm dating. This time, it was just a coincidence that I was talking with my mother right before you walked into that restaurant and changed my life. There was no hiding from it afterward; she always had too many questions about you.

I hung up the phone in tears because I could no longer talk with my parents. It hurt so much. Since my parents speak very limited English, I was excited to hear you talk in Portuguese with them and be fully integrated into my childhood home.

I guess that was my problem. I created this fantasy of us, the perfect picture. Then reality showed up, rocking its fists so hard that it made me learn that I had to build the proper foundation first. That or all of these dreams would fall down on top of me. Only me. You had already disappeared, leaving me alone to pick up the pieces and work on redesigning this fantasy again.

You learn from your failures, and I guess I can consider this a failure. This breakup made me realize how needy and codependent I am. You were always the star of my dreams and aspirations in life. It made me realize how much of my mother I have become over the years. If only I had realized this sooner, maybe you would still be here.

I need to learn to stop reproducing her behavior only because it's what is familiar to me. I need to become my own realized person, my own version of the perfect guy for myself. Maybe if you see that I'm working on myself, we can reunite and create a stronger relationship than before.

*Hey, I had such a crazy day, and I wish I could have told you all about it.*

After an insane day today, I wish we could go back to the old times when I would share every single detail about my day with you. You wouldn't have believed it! Unfortunately, you will never know about it, but I wish you could. I know you would have loved the thrill of it all.

Back when we were together, you would listen to me talk about my crazy days. In return, I would hug you after one of your stressful days. You worked a lot, and for long hours, so you often felt tired and defeated. You wouldn't be in the mood to talk, and you preferred a comforting hug instead. We had such an ideal dynamic, and I wish we could dive back into it once again.

Today, when I got to work, there was an unusual sense of chaos and energy. My colleagues quickly told me that the gossip was extraordinary and that I had to make logging into Slack (the software my company uses for communication) a priority. I was intrigued! I speed walked to my desk and turned on my laptop to open the Slack channel everyone was talking about: "Celebrate."

I was in disbelief when I opened that channel with over five thousand employees in it. People filled it with several crazy messages and metaphors. Some posts congratulated the higher-ups on their hefty bonuses when their salary increase didn't match inflation. Some others also compared it to how the union had been demanding a base salary that the board rejected several times—the same board that had been seeing substantial increases in their salaries year after year.

My company had just released its reported earnings, and once the union got a hold of it, the rest of the company was discontent with it. Everyone was in battle mode, and the whole company was on fire. Since all these employees were part of a union, they felt safe posting those things. I was on a different team that wasn't part of the union, so I was too anxious to even like one message for fear of being added to an internal blacklist. Unlike your coffee, this tea was burning hot!

Out of desperation, Human Resources tried to post a video of a cinnamon roll recipe, trying to steer the conversation in the opposite direction, but it was fruitless. (Figuratively and literally speaking! It would be an abomination if cinnamon rolls had raisins.)

After all that morning drama, I was getting ready to leave my office since I had a conference after lunch. Suddenly, another issue appeared. One of the social media channels we use for advertisement stopped all our marketing campaigns. A very unusual policy flag got triggered, something that should never have been an issue in the first place. Without getting too technical, this problem had no easy fix. It was a mess in need of a quick solution!

Once I got to the conference, I was busy trying to juggle dealing with that issue and paying attention to what was being presented. At some point, one of the speakers made a joke that had me cackling. That's when I saw a little head pop out of the row of seats across the aisle. To my surprise, I spotted one of my old coworkers who is now a friend. What? She was also there! She immediately recognized my distinct laughter and turned around to try to find me.

Not only wasn't I counting on her to be there, but I had also been texting her that morning to see if she was free to hang out that weekend. It was a true coincidence.

We ended up catching up after the conference and sharing some stories while laughing. It was indeed a rollercoaster of a day.

At least on a roller coaster, someone always comes to lift the safety equipment after the ride is over. There is someone checking on you to make sure you are alright at the end of the journey. Do you miss that feeling? Because I do. I wish you still texted me to ask about my day and see if everything was fine or if something crazy had happened.

Would you still be here to check in on me after work if I hadn't suffocated you with all my messages? Nowadays, I know you wanted some space after your busy workdays to unwind by yourself, but you never communicated that with me. You only told me *after* you broke up with me. If you had told me that before, I would have given you more space to breathe. I was unaware of how my actions hurt you, but now that I know, why don't we work together and try to fix it? We can do it. I have faith in our love.

I do wish for a lot of things, right? I guess I will never be satisfied with what I have and will always want more. I'll be forever stuck in this losing game, and I can't seem to break free from it. I think that what hurts me the most is knowing you would have loved to hear about my day. You loved this type of gossip, especially because it involved a union. I remember how pro-unions you are, and I think about the one you were trying to create at work. One of the last things I heard about it was that there would be some type of voting to implement it.

Can we use that as an excuse to talk again? I can ask you to tell me more about it as it motivated you so much. Then we can use it as an excuse to talk about our stories. I'm curious to know if your mom is still wearing your union pin, even though she lives in another state and no one around her will make any sense of it.

I want to hear your life updates, and most importantly, I want to hear your voice. I want to experience that feeling again. That feeling of knowing you're smiling on the other end of the line, even though it's just a normal phone call.

*Hey, I want you to know that I see it now. I'm sorry, I screwed up, too.*

During this journey to understand myself and heal from bad relationship patterns that keep repeating themselves over and over again, I have been doing some reading. I finished the relationship book I bought the other day, or should I say I devoured it. It opened my eyes so much that I couldn't put down *It's Not Me, It's You* after I started it.

While reading it, I was able to get in touch with the harm I did to you and the harm you did to me. I understood the damage we both did to the relationship. It does take two to tango, and we were stepping on each other's feet while we were still learning how to dance. The biggest difference is that my codependent anxious personality was still holding your hand while your hyper-independent avoidant personality was asking for a five-minute cigarette break. A break you wanted to take although you didn't smoke. A break where you realize you don't have cigarettes with you because you don't smoke. A break that would make you think that you need to go home to rest. A break that would leave your partner stranded, tangoing alone with nothing but their own shadow. A shadow that can't be held.

Through the pain, I was able to find a place where I don't hold grudges against you. I no longer prosecute you or see you as the villain. I have come to the conclusion that I screwed up, too. I'm no victim of this game, no matter how much I want to believe it.

You were still fighting your own demons, which some people like to describe as abandonment issues. You would rather cast someone away from your life than be vulnerable to the possibility of being heartbroken once again. And I would rather fight for someone and be anxious, chasing them down the rainiest of paths because that was the most romantic thing someone could do, regardless of how toxic it was.

My view made me feel like I was living in one of those romance movies, your favorite style. That's why, although I sensed you pulling away from me, I tried even harder. My need to feel loved was stronger. Stronger than your boundaries. Stronger than what any healthy relationship would say.

I ended up giving you my one hundred and fifty percent, not my one hundred and ten percent. This, in turn, made you feel scared because you weren't matching my level of effort. You felt as though you weren't good enough for me. You thought that I deserved someone who could equal my playing field, and you were sad you couldn't be that person. Work was just too demanding for you to dedicate yourself to love.

You see, I'm not the ideal person. I don't have my life put together like you thought I did. We are all imperfect. We are never ready for love because we will perpetually be lost. The difference is that I was ready to keep you company while we figured out what life is all about, figuring out our problems and the best solutions.

I wanted to create a safe space where we could flourish and challenge each other. In five years, neither of us will be the same, compared to who we are today. It's all about how we lift each other's spirits and allow that growth to happen in synchrony. It will be at different paces, but it will always be together. Until our hearts stop beating. Until our hands don't have the strength to hold one another anymore. Until, unknowingly, we text "over" for the last time.

I do realize now that my codependency was out of control. I needed some help, and through all this suffering, you were the one who opened my eyes. You see, funnily enough, codependency started being studied in the wives of alcoholics, which came as a surprise to me. I was about to move in with an alcoholic before I met you. We jump from relationship to relationship to ease the pain and the loneliness in our souls. Self-love feels like a distant dream, scattered toward infinity. According to this definition, I'm struggling.

That's why I wanted to start dating again that same day you left me. To ease the pain. But in opposition to what you told me the night you broke up with me—*I deserved someone who could match and give me the attention and love I needed and deserved because I was so wonderful*—I don't need that. That behavior was just my inability to tune in with my true self. The yells from my codependent thoughts silenced my inner voice, and they didn't allow anything else to voice their opinions.

I thought I needed someone who would be there at any given moment because I was unhappy when I was alone. I mean . . . I still am. I'm dissatisfied with myself, and because of that, I was demanding more than what you could give me. The reality is that I need to change this thought, or I will keep seeking validation from others.

Against every single voice of that burning desire to get back into dating, I made a hard vow not to jump into the dating scene. I know it will be tough, but I must heal myself first and learn how to love myself. After that, I can find a person who will complement me, not someone whose main job is to replace the void I feel inside.

It may seem like I'm contradicting myself when I said we are never ready for love and that the magic happens when you grow with someone. The truth is that I'm a mess right now, and the starting foundation needs some stability I don't currently possess. So, in the most anticlimactic way, thank you for showing this side of me that I desperately needed to see.

The reason why that relationship book opened my eyes was because it told a story about two therapists in love, and it felt like our story. One was anxious and the other was avoidant. They both had different views of what it meant to be *the one*. Another important element was the fact that they were both damaged. I saw our actions in it, and I could easily swap the characters with us. It was all so crystal clear that it made me aware of my flaws.

As I was approaching the end of it, hope started to take over me again. I thought that this book could also make you see the truth. Suddenly, I was infused with this urge to give it to you. It described the problems with having fantasies about *the one* so perfectly. It contradicted your deep desire to believe in that one person who will show up on a foggy night and be the Mr. Right. All these illusions that one day you will experience a Hallmark movie fantasy have poisoned you.

It's okay to have conflict and disagreements. In my world, through all the imperfections, I could still see the bigger picture with you in it. A person I would spend hours and hours talking and laughing with. Someone I had great chemistry with. Someone I enjoyed spending time with. Most importantly, someone whose values I sought in a partner and who would make me a better person in the long run. In other words, YOU.

Because of that, no matter how many imperfections you had, you were still worth fighting for. You are *the one* for me.

I can't lie, I was desperate for you to read the self-help book. There was this delusion in me that wanted to keep fighting for you and make you realize that we are both perfectly imperfect.

I had this belief that if we could swim through the first wave, we could enjoy the calm ocean our lives could hypothetically be. All we had to do first was to realize our problems so we could fight them together. I was so desperate to keep fighting for you like the codependent idiot that I am; so desperate for love that . . . I texted you after I finished reading it.

I wrote that I wanted to give you the book because it resonated with me and I saw our struggles in it. I told you how it opened my eyes and made me realize I had some healing to do. I also told you that I wanted to apologize for my actions and that I felt that the therapists' lessons could also benefit you. It could help you understand yourself, so you could prepare for whomever was in store for you in the future. I didn't tell you this part, but I hoped it would be me. I want you to be happy, but I want you to be the happiest with me.

As my feelings and emotions are in turmoil inside of me, one thing remains constant. I'm the world's most terrible liar. My actions today showed that, at the end of the day, I still haven't learned anything about my healing journey.

*Hey, I just got home from having the most interesting dinner.*

A friend of mine and I decided that we should start the night at a restaurant in Brooklyn before heading out to a birthday party. Little did I know that seeing him would be the most gut-wrenching experience I had exposed myself to lately.

For starters, when I greeted him at the restaurant, I noticed he was wearing a flannel shirt, just like you. He was going to Brooklyn after all. Although you were only a few years older than me, you had this endearing way of calling yourself the Oldest Man in Bushwick, the neighborhood in Brooklyn where I lived. Because of that, you had a habit of dressing like the locals who lived there to fit in. In your mind, that was flannel. That was an inside joke just for us since those were our memories. I only wanted to see you wearing flannel. Not him.

I sat across from him while he greeted me with a big smile. But that smile belonged to him. No matter how similar your clothes were, it didn't belong to you. I love my friend, but not as I loved you. All that I wished for, at that moment, was that you could switch spots with him for one last dinner. I would have prayed and made sacrifices for that opportunity.

Unfortunately, I don't think the entity above us listens to me. I had tried to pray the gay away when I was younger, and it was unsuccessful. Why would it be any different now? I wish there was a way; I had so much hunger for reconnecting with you over dinner that I wouldn't mind if all we ate was mint chocolate chip ice cream. That's how desperate I was.

As I sat down, my mind raced, trying to find in him that warmth I felt when I used to see you grin, that happiness so uniquely yours. I looked away to try to shake that thought out of my head and shifted my focus to the staircase next to me.

They were decorated with plants and Christmas lights, from the first step all the way to the last one. If I was already missing you, thinking that this restaurant was exactly your style was the death of me. I had no idea that the place I picked was so romantic.

Deep inside me, there was this craving to take you there the next day. I desired to see your smile once again, like you would when I showed you an interesting new adventure you weren't expecting.

That wish became stronger when I hoped my friend would extend his hand for me to hold across the table while we looked at the menu. I waited in anticipation for that kiss on the back of my hand when we were both done deciding what to eat. Unfortunately, that was my story with *you,* not him.

Realizing that it was a friend of mine in front of me and not you didn't make the pain less real. If only I had the opportunity to see you again, maybe then you would see how much I love you and am willing to fight for you. I want to tell you I screwed up and am keen to improve myself. Maybe, as a bonus, we would get another free Diet Coke because you winked at the server by accident, like it happened before.

This wound became even more crushing when my friend expressed his desire to leave the city. Fortunately, you will never know how hard I was fighting the tears at that table. All I wanted was to excuse myself so I could cry in the bathroom. But I couldn't. I had to sit there and let him express his frustrations and the pain he was feeling. I couldn't believe one more person was leaving me.

Toward the end, he mentioned how he noticed my emotional state and how uncomfortable it made him feel to see me so destroyed inside. That was the reason why he wasn't able to look me in the eyes—similarly to you when you ended our love story. My eyes are up here, and they are hurting. Why do you keep avoiding them?

When you said our relationship was over, all I wanted was to run away from the city, start my life anew, and break free from the heartbreak. All I wanted was to simply run away from my feelings, without even resolving them. Instead, I tried to find support from my group of friends, but how could I do that if they were moving away? They were also escaping from their own demons and the city. It felt like someone had pulled the rug from under me. All of a sudden, I was falling without knowing how deep the drop would be. The only thing that I could hold on to was myself. But what was the point of holding my own hand when all of me was free falling down the hole?

When we left the restaurant, all I wanted was for you to be there for me. To put your arm around me, kiss my forehead, and say, "It's okay. You once left your friends back home to move to New York. It's okay for them to do the same. Love is also letting go."

The reality is that it's difficult to let go of either of you. Both of you had been my support. Doing it and relearning to fight battles by myself is hard. It's as hard as it's to put on a fake smile; like the one I put on while we headed to our next stop, the birthday party.

I hadn't been counting on being the first to arrive and having every seat available. I'm never that early to get the privilege of deciding which empty seat to take. We decided to claim a booth by a corner in the back. I sat on the bench against the wall, and naturally, my friend sat across from me on a stool. No matter how much I yearned for it, he wasn't you, and therefore he wasn't going to sit next to me. He wasn't motivated to sit as close to me as possible, in a spot where our legs could meet, his hand could meet mine, and we could kiss whenever we so desired.

Throughout the night, more people showed up, but no one ever sat next to us. They would come in and sit by the entrance while we were alone at the very back of the bar, far away from everyone. It brought me back to our first date at that arcade bar, where no one would get close to us because of our chemistry. No one dared to get closer to us as the air surrounding us was filled with sparks flying in every direction. It was clear that afternoon was ours. In parallel, this night didn't belong to my friend and me. It belonged to the birthday boy, and we were mere spectators in his night.

Eventually, I told my friend how much I miss you and the jealousy I feel when I see a couple holding hands. How we could have fought for a future together and built such a beautiful one. We were so promising. If only we had fought a little harder, I believe we could have made it.

Instead, I was there, sitting in that booth, feeling so lonely. With teary eyes because you will forever be a distant and unreachable dream. No one would be there dancing our dance. You were unique. You were special.

But this friend who once pushed me to go on that first date with you was now telling me his thoughts without skipping a beat. *You weren't ready for a relationship. We shouldn't fight for unavailable people, as that will only lead to disappointment. You had to put in some work before we were both ready to try again. We shouldn't fall in love with the potential that someone might have.* The potential someone has is a false reality we hold on to.

I'm not going to lie, although I resonated with the harsh truths he said, I also couldn't deny how I still want you. I was ready to wait in the uncertainty. Would you ever come back to me? Would you ever reach your potential and prove him wrong?

I didn't mind giving it time while you worked your things out and I worked on mine. I'm no saint either. The burden shouldn't be all on you.

It still hurts me. I was hoping we could develop our own personas together as couples do. The question now invading my mind was whether there was a way to fight destiny. Perhaps there is a way for us to flip the script. I'm still in love with your potential, and I can't let the thought of you go.

In the end, my friend and I parted ways. This time around, I knew I would see him again before he left the city. At least there was that certainty warming me as I walked the cold path back home, missing the comfort of your touch on my shoulder, keeping me warm, and reassuring me that loving is also letting go.

# Step Four:

# Depression

Day Twenty-Four

*Hey, I was cleaning my closet today and saw my ugly Christmas sweaters.*

People say that doing chores is the best way to distract your mind, especially if you hate them. Your brain tunes into a different frequency and pushes aside the thoughts you're busy trying to camouflage. That was why I took on the mission of cleaning my closet today. Little did I know that, shortly after I embarked on this mission, I would have to hold my small collection of ugly Christmas sweaters. There weren't that many since my goal is to buy a new one every year, until one year I have enough to wear a different one every day in December. As I held them in my hands, I wondered if you still remember that date.

We had agreed to bar hop, and while I prepared for that night, I had this brilliant idea. It could have either been super romantic or a big flashy red flag. I was unsure if it was the right move or not since it was only our second date. Although uncertainty clouded me, I still decided to gamble and go with it. Luckily it paid off.

On your way to my neighborhood in Brooklyn for our date, I texted you asking if you were wearing flannel again. Since you wanted to blend in the last time you came to my area, I wondered if you would do that again.

As I had expected, you replied in the affirmative way. You even attached the most adorable selfie. I was in disbelief when I noticed that you were wearing red and green, already representing the Christmas colors. You truly wanted to take its spirit wherever you went, like an elf spreading the season's magic with every step you took. That was why I decided to wear an ugly Christmas sweater that night, so we could both cheer for the same team.

We started our night at a charismatic bar in Bushwick with funky decor that matched its eccentric vibe: Boobie Trap. After that, we would barhop around until we reached the last one on my list. I had saved the best for last.

When you got to the first bar, I was already there with an insane plan in my mind. The first step was praying you wouldn't find it too crazy. The second one consisted of me saying, "Ew, I don't like your clothes." I still laugh when I think about the distress on your face. You were in disbelief.

I then turned around to grab another ugly Christmas sweater that I handed to you. I can't forget the look on your face as you grabbed it. What was once a surprised look was now a beaming face, excited to put it on right away. I told you then that I was only letting you borrow one of mine, not giving it to you, so I didn't sound too crazy. That was the moment I realized a problem with my plan.

On our second date, we were already wearing matching clothes, like a couple opening presents in their pajamas on Christmas Day. Not only were we both celebrating this holiday, but both of us were wearing festive green and red sweaters. The issue was that I only had three sweaters. One of them was blue with Jesus and Santa riding a shark, which could have been too much for someone whose views of religion I didn't fully grasp. So that left me with my other two, which were both green and red but more family-friendly. The one I was wearing had a dog with a Santa hat and three small bells on the dog's collar. The one you were wearing had some tacos wrapped up with a bow. I decided you should have that one because you had recently returned from spending four years in Los Angeles.

Thankfully, my plan was a hit. You loved wearing it as we hopped from bar to bar, exploring the area.

Looking back at it, it's no wonder that people thought you and I were a couple. We had an unmatched chemistry, evident in the passionate kisses we traded, the laughter we shared, and most importantly, our matching sweaters. It was such a fun date, and it made me want to spend as much time with you as possible. You were wonderful, and it's futile to try to describe how well we matched. We just did. Not only was I enjoying spending time with you, but I was coming to realize that your values also aligned with mine and you would challenge me to be a better person. You were exactly what I was looking for. My early Christmas gift.

The bar I saved for last was the one I knew you would love the most. It was this tiki bar filled with Christmas lights, sparkling garlands, and drinks that came in festive glasses. Since each drink had an associated cup, every time we fin-ished our drinks, we would rush to the bar to try a new one.

We wanted to try them all! There was a snowman, a ginger-bread man, a Santa, and . . . a mismatched flamingo floatie? It was a bar dedicated to Christmas. But I saw it as a place dedicated to you.

If only I had taken a photo of your face that night so I could relive it whenever I wanted to. I hadn't seen that much excitement in a long time. It was a precious memory that was mine and yours. It was only ours.

It was the beginning of our story. It was one of those moments when you know the other person is *the one*. Even though they are only two inches taller than you and struggle when they try to put their arm around your shoulders while walking down the street.

After a while, the only cups we hadn't experimented with were the ones that came with hot drinks. We decided to ask for them, no matter how abrupt the change would be. We wanted to make the most out of our night.

When we went back to our table, we took a sip before we looked at each other. We were sharing the same thought: a spiked hot drink would kill the night. It would likely make us feel sleepy, an outcome we didn't want. We wanted to live in each other's essence for as long as the night would take us.

Without hesitation, we put our drinks down and started doing the previous Monday's New York Times Crossword. I had been telling you how I liked doing them, but that they sometimes were too hard for me. I don't get a lot of references and clues since I didn't grow up in the United States. On the other hand, you hadn't done them in the longest time, and you wanted to give it a shot. So, we sat side by side cuddling on a couch at the bar with my phone between us. Trying to figure out the answers to each clue. Using kisses as incentives for getting something right. We were able to beat it quite fast, and you were feeling very proud of yourself. Up to the point where you said we had to do it more often until you could finish it faster than one of your friends.

I hope you haven't forgotten about that bar. That you still remember the stranger who came up to us to talk about our undisputed chemistry. I hope you still think about all the magic we created that night.

I know that the bar is far from your apartment and that you will probably never wind up there to relive the glory of that night. I can only hope that one day you stumble upon the video you took of the tiki bar that made you starstruck. That looking at the place where we fell in love makes you think of me.

There is no way of me knowing what you are up to. To know if you still miss me or if you're trying to move on, forgetting about me by burying yourself in work or in another person.

All I can say is, wherever you are, please don't let all those crazy good moments we spent together leave your memory. Remember the sound that the bells from my Christmas sweater made whenever you would pull me in for a kiss.

*Hey, I finally burned that winter candle.*

Do you remember the candle that sat in the middle of my round wooden dining table? The one that smelled like winter. The one that smelled like you. It had this wintery aroma to it of fresh pines or, in other words, of *Christmas trees*. It made my apartment smell like an everlasting Christmas, and I loved every part of it. In my mind, it was like I could bring you back with the simple gesture of lighting a candle. On a daily basis, I was able to relive your existence through my memories, but smelling it activated one of my five senses, making the masterpiece that my brain was creating even more powerful.

As the candle's wick burnt down to the very bottom, I couldn't help but wonder if you had ever finished burning your Christmas candles. It was one of your last questions before breaking up with me. You wanted to know if you should burn all of yours or save them for next year. You had collected so many of them over time because you treasured the coziness they provided. To you, the ideal home would be made of only candles and pillows. It would be a place where the air conditioner would be set to a freezing temperature, where you could only enter if you had a cozy cashmere sweater on.

You loved them so much that you even collected this beautiful candle that was displayed on top of your coffee table. It was a bust of Kesha. Yes, the pop star! It was merely decorative since you didn't want to ruin its design by lighting it. You adored it for the visual, not for the smell.

I hope you thought the same of me when I woke up next to you in the morning. That you wanted me for who I was, regardless of my morning breath. Loving someone for who they are without the glitz and glamour is part of what love is.

This story is very reminiscent of a show we both loved so dearly that it bonded us right away, *Happy Endings*. It was incredible how we couldn't stop quoting it! We even had this little game between us where we would try to find a scene from the show to describe any situation. We had finally found a game you liked, and we could always succeed at it. One time, when a friend of mine complained about how she hated that her birthday fell on New Year's Eve, we suggested she lie about the date. She could pretend that she had a summer birthday instead. Just like it happened in one episode.

Out of the endless number of scenes that could describe my current emotional state, the most relevant ones revolve around this hopeless romantic main character who is someone I share so much with. We are both desperately afraid of dying alone.

During her thirtieth birthday, after one more unsuccessful date, she proclaimed that she was going to die alone in a light-up Christmas sweater. I hope that this isn't a foreshadowing of my future. I hate the thought of spending my birthday next year saying those exact same words while wearing the Christmas sweater you wore on our second date. Reminiscing about that night as I make my birthday wish.

There was also an episode with an important scene revolving around a candle. This comically unlovable character was now in a relationship and had received a giant candle on Christmas from her boyfriend. Her friend thought it was a weird gift that lacked personality when, in reality, she loved it. Before that, she had a conversation with her partner after watching a sad movie where he said to her that if she was dying, he wouldn't let her suffer like the character. He would put a bullet in her head and light the biggest candle he could find to match her big heart.

If I associated the smell of that candle with the essence of you, does burning it to the end mean our love has died? What happens when there is nothing to shine a light upon our present and future?

It's also interesting how that candle episode highlighted another character as well, the self-proclaimed *gift whisperer*. Someone who thought they gave the best presents when they weren't what the person really wanted. In hindsight, all my small gifts to you might have felt like that. What you needed was space, but without communication, I ended up giving you the opposite. I started to sense you slipping away and tried my best to bring you closer. I felt so anxious that I was going to lose you that I tried my best to make you come back. This led me to try to surprise you countless times, with different plans and small gifts. If only back then you had communicated with me about how you were feeling. That you felt like you had to match my efforts and were pressured because you felt like you couldn't.

Nowadays, our candle already ran its course. There is nothing left of it.

Is it me, or is the best match made of two lonely people? They will fully commit to one another and smother each other in appreciation so they don't lose the other person. I guess that's what I did. Perhaps I was too lonely and sad until your smile warmed my heart. Like a candle that slowly fades away because it's too close to the window, where the sun shines bright. Slowly melting, although no one ever lit the wick. Just the course of time slowly fading away what was once such a beautiful candle.

*Hey, today I had the most delicious mac and cheese pizza.*

You know how everyone has their comfort food, something that will always bring them happiness? Something that's usually associated with their childhood or home state/country? It's interesting how my comfort food isn't a traditional dish from back home. Instead, it's one of the most American dishes someone can think of—a good mac and cheese.

That's why when I saw the combination of this dish with pizza, I knew I had to try it. I ordered a slice at a pizza joint before meeting my group of friends at a bar. We usually just hang out with drinks weekly since I don't care that much about food.

I have never been a huge fan of food because my parents have tainted that relationship for me. I view food as a synonym for fighting, distrust, and the source of all the problems that happened during my childhood. My dad found comfort in overeating and would use it as an escape mechanism from his issues. He would devour his troubles away with a big meal, gaining other problems, or, more precisely, weight. A lot of it. It started to become a big issue for my parents.

I wonder how my mother ever sleeps since my dad has this snore you can hear from across the apartment. Even if there are three rooms in between. That snore is associated with his obesity, and at some point, a doctor said that he could die at any moment in his sleep due to a bad case of sleep apnea. He was still unable to stop overeating and gaining weight until he had to have surgery. Thanks to it, he lost a lot of weight, but that was a Band-Aid, not a solution for his challenges. With time, he started stress eating again since he never tackled the problem from its core. My mother, in turn, decided to oversee and control everything he ate. She would shame him for going for seconds and try to find him snacking late at night. This was my first introduction to codependency as a child and it impacted how I perceive relationships.

My mother's emotions are based on my dad's relationship with food. While I was growing up, she was constantly unhappy because of his weight, and those recurring fights would dim her light. She was unable to detach from his addiction because she thought she could change him.

If successful, she would finally feel accomplished. It felt like her main mission in life was to make sure she managed the calories he ate. However, my dad would get frustrated with the constant nagging and would eat even more. His method of dealing with frustrations was still to have a big meal. This cycle would never end since my mother would then become frustrated. He wasn't paying attention to her needs, and she ended up miserable, only associating her feelings with my dad's relationship with food.

You can call it trauma, but the reality is that I don't care about food because of it. I never put too much thought into what I eat. Without strong preferences around this topic, we were able to mix well when it came time to pick a restaurant or food. You were vegetarian and, to me, it's all the same. Food is just food. It's not something that brings me peace or comfort. And it will never be love. Just a necessity.

Nevertheless, mac and cheese always made me feel like I was on cloud nine, without it being associated with a single memory. It was purely my love for pasta and cheese.

This lack of preferences leads me to say yes to anything, as I'm rarely in the mood for some specific type of food. That's why you were so shocked the first time you cooked for me. I had already cooked for you several times because I saw it providing you pleasure. I would cook you a true continental breakfast that would blow your mind whenever you spent the night at my place, in true Club Med Brooklyn fashion.

I used to joke that one day I would give you a punch card so that you could get a free breakfast on the tenth stay. I'm not sure if, once again, you felt the pressure to retribute the favor and match me, but when it came your time to prepare a meal, you were unsure of what to do. The fact that you didn't have a lot of ingredients in your apartment didn't help.

That was when I spotted something on your shelf that sparked my interest. "I would love some mac and cheese," I told you. I was met, once again, with another surprised and confused look, as if I was a box of mysteries to you. You never knew what to expect. You were intrigued since it was the opposite of what I would do for you at my apartment.

I like to believe that I'm low maintenance and not that fancy. I didn't need you to cook for one hour to show your appreciation for me. Especially since that's one hour I don't get to cuddle with you while watching a movie. For that reason, I told you that we should make something simple and focus on enjoying each other's company.

I wish I could forever relive that hug on your couch after we ate your food. All I wanted was to maximize those scarce hours we would have for ourselves during the week. They were endearing to me since we only had time to properly hang out on weekends.

That night, you fell asleep on top of me, and when the morning came, you told me how much that moment meant to you. You expressed how important it was for you to feel comfortable around me. You were able to surrender yourself to sleep with your head on my chest while watching a movie. Those words were magic to my ears. It's an incredible feeling to be someone's comfort food in a way, to have the ability to make them feel at ease and euphoric.

In true comfort food fashion, all those memories of us came to my mind from a simple bite of that pizza. Carbs on carbs, with some melted cheese on top. Yet, it was powerful enough to awaken many hidden desires. The funny thing is that I could see myself in that slice. Curled up in sadness like a macaroni drenched in cheese, melting like the emotions that overcame me.

All I craved at that moment was for you to still be with me so I could let you have a bite of my slice. If you weren't there,

I would ask for a to-go portion so I could see your face of happiness when experiencing this incredible pizza. Savoring all these flavors by myself was a complicated task when I could only think of that primal desire to share that experience with you. The realization that you no longer exist in my life is a hard reality to face.

In a weirdly metaphorical way, pizzas are like relationships. You fall in love with the finished product, but you don't quit on it while it's still baking in the oven. You always wait for it to finish cooking. Only then do you decide whether to keep it or toss it into the trash because it's burnt. All the little ingredients are the things that make your partner unique. Apart they mean nothing; they need the base, the foundation of the relationship. When everything goes into the oven, that's when people grow together. Blending all the flavors into one.

Love is a work in progress. It's the decision of standing there while waiting for it to be ready and finally being able to relish all the hard work. Maybe this is why you had no ingredients when you cooked for me. Maybe you weren't that great of a cook. Maybe that's why you decided to leave the kitchen before waiting for things to improve.

I wish the ending to our story never happened. I wanted to be able to explore new restaurants and live new experiences with you. Instead, I left the pizza store with my emotions as raw as an uncooked pizza. I felt alone and incomplete.

*Hey, last night I was invited to the same drag brunch we went to that one time.*

One of my friends proposed going to it since he wanted to support the drag queen hosting it. He was also craving their steak, but it was easier to convince me to go to brunch for the drag queens than for the food.

It so happens to be the same one we went to on our sixth date. Or maybe it was the eighth? I can't remember. We had this theory that if you spent the night at my apartment, it would count as one and a half dates, so sometimes it was hard to keep track of the numbers. All I know is that it was a date. Another five-star date.

I'm nervous about this brunch, though. I fear looking at the table where we once sat and envisioning ourselves there. Sitting like lunatics, side by side, at a table for four since it was the only way for both of us to see the show.

I wonder if I will think about the moment when you looked at your phone and randomly said, "Guess my mom is also at a drag brunch. She must have been bored at home." That woman was a mystery to me, and I adored the picture I had of her.

I'm also not sure if this time I will take the last bite of my food and find a shard of glass like I did when I was with you. That occurrence was such a crucial moment in getting to know each other. There's glass in the food—how should we react? Should we politely notify the server or be rude because we could have gotten hurt? Are we going to demand the item be free because it was unsafe? In the sea of possibilities, the answer didn't surprise me. I didn't see a new side of you, and we were both always so calm in every situation. We dealt with this problem in such a graceful way that the server gave us a cocktail free of charge. Bless! We were such a good pair.

That date was still before I had gone home for my Christmas break, when our relationship was still green, like the Christmas sweater you wore on the second date. Thinking about it brings back so many sweet memories that I would rather not think about while I'm trying to have fun with my friends. That date meant a lot to me because it allowed me to discover new sides of you. New quirks, as I like to call them.

After some cups of coffee and cocktails, as everyone does, I had this urge to use the bathroom. When I got back, I was surprised to see an unfamiliar lady next to our table with a basket of Christmas goodies lying on top of it.

When I arrived, you quickly asked me if I had cash on me. Assuming you were heavily interested in what she had to sell, without any hesitation, I gave you a twenty-dollar bill. There are things you don't question when someone's passion sits right in front of them.

I used to collect everything Simpsons-related when I was younger, so I understood passions. Walking into my bedroom in the seventh grade felt like the comedy relief of any rom-com. I had a Bart Simpson duvet, a ceiling light that featured him on the glass dome, a blanket with the whole family on top of a bean bag, shelves filled with books and merchandise, and more. There were never enough Simpsons in my life, not even when there was a limited collection inside of Kinder Surprise (sorry, Americans). I was so determined to collect all of them that I got physically sick from eating too much chocolate. I was never able to get the last missing figurine for my collection. That was the first time I quit on a goal because I couldn't do it any longer.

I understood you. If buying Christmas trinkets was your source of happiness, I would never say no.

After your purchase, she swiftly left, and I will never forget how you cursed the wind with an adorable smile. You were in disbelief at how gullible you could be. You told me how, while I was away, the lady entered the bar and went straight to the table with the person she knew wouldn't be able to say no. Her plan worked.

You felt bad for her after she presented you with what she had to sell. You also couldn't say you didn't have any cash because we clearly had singles on our table to tip the drag queens. But you also happened not to have any cash on you. That was when I returned from the bathroom to save the interaction. I didn't want to deny you the gratification of getting some chocolate spoons, Christmas cards, candy, and some Christmas trinkets! Little did I know that you weren't that fond of your purchase! What?

You sat there in disbelief at how naïve you had been. From my perspective, I thought it had been a sweet showing of your character. How the Christmas magic followed you wherever you went. Probably that lady only saw one person wearing a Christmas sweater and went straight to them. She knew that person loved the season and would be an easy target.

So early in the dating stages, people can look at these things and think not being able to say no is a negative trait or a red flag. I saw these traits of yours as endearing. They were the stupid things that made you who you were, and who you were was who I adored.

After that brunch, we headed to a bar where another drag queen hosted a game day. She was a friend of mine, and she had previously hosted a drag brunch at a different establishment. I was scared of committing "drag brunch treason" and having her see me on Instagram at this other restaurant, so I felt the need to go there and say hi to her. Although you weren't a gamer, I was still able to convince you to come with me. I knew we could easily grab a seat at the bar while other people played video games on the TV.

When we arrived, I introduced you to this friend who traditionally wears a mop as a wig. She has been around my life for years, and she has met all the guys I have dated since I moved to the United States.

Knowing her for that long has its perks and detriments. One of the latter is that I know most of her repertoire. I know what song she likes to use to start her shows and some of the most popular segments. One of them always happens during Christmas time.

She is originally from Ohio and, over there, she grew up with the classic Christmas song, "I Want a Hippopotamus for Christmas." After moving to New York, she was surprised to find a cult following over the song, "Dominick the Donkey," especially among people who grew up in New Jersey. Every single time she would bring up this story, someone in the audience would burst in excitement because they knew this song. That time it had been you.

You got out of your chair and went next to the stage to sing the song, close to the microphone she was holding, with one hand inside your pocket, your Christmas sweater on, and a beautiful smile on your face. You looked so mesmerizing at that moment, defending your love for that festive song even though some people said that they didn't like it. You looked so perfect that I had to take a video of it to remember that moment forever. That was the video I would show people when they asked me about you and what you looked like. It was also that video of you that I later showed to my mother. I was so proud of those fifteen seconds I recorded while I admired you from a distance, as it captured the essence of who you are. The man I was so in awe of, my very own "Italian Christmas Donkey."

Later that day, I got a text from that drag queen saying that she was happy I was finally moving on from my previous partner. She liked you!

What a magical way to wrap up that day. It was truly another incredible date that solidified how special you were to me. Thanks to it, I will never think of stale-ass Italian cookies and "Dominick the Donkey" without thinking of you, of how adorable you looked describing that childhood experience of yours to the microphone while nervously laughing. Talking with a spark in your eyes. The type of spark you wish you could catch like a firefly to then put inside a bottle for safekeeping. This way, you can always wear it like a necklace next to your heart. Jingling like a Christmas bell.

*Hey, today I walked by the street where we had our last date.*

It was hard to stand there and watch couples walk by, thinking that we were one of them at some point. After destiny played its tricks on me, I was left recollecting all our memories from that day, like pieces of a puzzle scattered across that street. I felt sad we would never have another chance to finish our story. To me, you were a full book in need of a sequel. I wonder if, to you, I only meant a single chapter in the story you call your life.

I figure that all this hurt is my fault. The reason why so many places on that street remind me of you is because I took you to four different places in one day. I hadn't seen you in two weeks, and I took on the mission of planning a date where we would go to all your favorite spots, places I knew would make you smile.

I searched online for what to do around a specific area of the city I wanted to show you, and our starting location ended up being the New York Transit Museum. A funny coincidence because, unknowingly to me, you loved trains! I wasn't counting on this museum giving you a dose of serotonin since you had a hidden passion for trains and subways.

Although you loved that museum, I can't express to you how bored I was there. I didn't have the patience to read all those little plaques. There was so much information about the different types of rocks, the length of tunnels, strikes and unions, the difference between all those train models . . . There was so much to read!

Naturally, my brain kept falling asleep whenever I tried to pay attention to something that required reading more than two lines of text. If I had been there by myself, I would have left in a heartbeat. However, you were having the time of your life, and I couldn't deny you that pleasure. In fact, seeing the joy on your face whenever you read a fun fact made me smile from ear to ear. You were ready to repeat it to me so I could learn as well. Thanks to that, I started looking at things differently. I felt happiness in a boring place.

Suddenly, I didn't mind waiting for you, even when I had already seen the next two rooms. I would trace my step back to lay my head on your shoulder while you read things that my brain didn't internalize. I had no desire to rush you. It was very captivating how every time I came back from seeing something else, you were ready to share a new fun fact that I had ignored. I simply wanted you to enjoy your time and do something fun after a long week at work.

I think that this is another part of what love is, not having to be entertained all the time. Even if you don't want to be somewhere, you're still able to cherish it thanks to the pleasure it brings the other person. I would also be lying if I said that I didn't get any joy from that museum. All because of what happened when we were in the gift shop.

I was in line to buy a model train, a gift for a family member, when you approached me very cheerfully.

"Did you see the jewelry section?" you asked me.

"Yes, I saw the handcuffs. They are adorable," I quickly replied, assuming I knew what you were talking about.

You then started laughing like no one's business, causing the cashier to give us an enigmatic look. I don't know if he heard me say anything since we were next in line or if it was purely your laugh. That was when you corrected me. You said that the right word was cufflinks, not handcuffs. That funny mistake made me join your train of laughs.

I don't think I ever told you this, but that was something I deeply appreciated about you.

As English isn't my first language, I often butcher a word or an expression, but you would never judge me. I would say crazy things that made no sense, and you would always find it *enduring*. I chose this word on purpose because, for the longest time, I kept thinking it was the correct spelling of *endearing*. You never corrected me. Not even once. You understood what I meant, and you had this rule that if the typo or error wasn't crazy enough to completely change the meaning of things, you would not correct the person. Unless it allowed for a brilliant pun such as the one you once made after I said, "I had five bears at the bar." You were so understanding, and I found you so irresistible for that.

That museum closed early in the afternoon, giving us plenty of time to walk to an unknown destination (after you were done reading through a million descriptions). You might have fancied the first spot by luck, but the next one was fully planned.

I knew you would adore stopping at an ice cream store, and I wasn't wrong. We hopped into a parlor with exotic flavors and unique toppings. I was anxious that you wouldn't try a new thing and, instead, pick that awful mint chocolate chip ice cream because I wanted to try your choice as well. I usually go for something similar to cookies and cream or cookie dough, but that time the quirky girl behind the counter convinced me to try their baklava ice cream. I was on a mission to explore new things, and it was always a fun adventure to make new memories by your side.

I usually devour my food in a few bites, and ice cream is not an exception to this rule. This makes it one of the worst types of food for me to have on a date because I usually get long, painful brain freezes as I wolf it down like there is no tomorrow. Nothing is sexier than looking at someone knowing they are hitting their head with their hand to try to thaw their brain.

Somehow, next to you, I barely got those annoying brain freezes. Your presence was so charming that it warmed me up inside. What I got to experience instead was us talking and talking about everything once again, laughing while we indulged in the time of our lives. I still can't believe how we always found a topic of conversation. We never had a boring moment, did we?

We darted out of that place because the clock was ticking, and we were in a rush to get to the next venue. Personally, the best part of that day was knowing you never had a clue of what to expect next. I loved seeing the excitement on your face whenever you were surprised. I had planned everything without telling you a single detail of the plan because you loved surprises.

So, much to my content, you were really confused by the next stop once we arrived at our destination. From the outside, surrounded by big buildings, the corner of the street looked like it held a small winter lodge. Once we got inside, you were mesmerized by their wooden interior that featured a fireplace and cabin décor. It felt like a resort bar at the end of a ski course. It was cozy and warm, unlike the harsh, frigid temperature outside that the city had to offer. I knew you would appreciate that wine bar.

We sat at a small table with barely any room for our drinks and the cheese board we ordered. That table was so wiggly that it was a menace and made me laugh. We had to constantly hold it down to not knock down our wine glasses. It didn't matter to us, though; we didn't need much to have a good time. Even the frustrations would make us crack a few jokes. That was more proof that every moment with you was special.

Out of all my memories from that day, I think that one was my favorite. Not only was that awful table not enough to ruin our mood, but I felt so complete and fuzzy next to you inside that small cabin. It made me wonder about future

Christmas getaways with you. It made me think of how nice it would be to share a glass of wine with you after a long day, in the comfort of our own house.

After more long hours of banter, and eventually having gone to another table that had freed up, we decided it was time to leave. Otherwise, we wouldn't have time to do the last activity for the night, a movie theater.

We thought about the one where we had seen *Gremlins* since it was a special place that allowed food and drinks. We looked at their selection of movies and picked one that sounded interesting when we judged it by its synopsis, but it was actually a hot mess. We might have been lost the whole time, but at least there was comfort in knowing that we weren't alone in our confusion. We had each other, a bottle of wine between us, and a sense of accomplishment after such a successful date.

Man . . . how special was that day? If I knew then it would be our last date, would I have changed anything? Would I have tried to do less to impress you, just picking one idea and letting it be all for the day? To be honest, I probably wouldn't have changed a thing because it was all so magical. Hindsight is a powerful thing; if only I knew then how you felt. The worst part is that no matter how often we would see each other, it was always the best time of my week. I always looked forward to seeing you again, week after week. You made me happier than anyone could. My face would hurt from smiling and laughing so hard for hours. My heart would be full as our hands intertwined.

You are the reason why so many romance movies are made. You are the muse for the most romantic lines in all of them. You are the inspiration for all those different ways of saying "I love you." Words that I never told you, in fear of you leaving me for moving too fast. But now that this fear is already a reality, I can finally say it without hesitation. *I love you.*

I hope you think about that last date, especially because, when you destroyed our love, you said you were afraid we didn't have enough in common. Instead of trying to find excuses to justify calling us *over*, because we were getting too involved and you were hesitant about having someone hurt you again, could you have stopped and looked at that day? What we had in common was so extraordinary and wonderful. We had enough mutual interests to spend a full day together in harmony.

I won't deny that we had some different interests, *yes*, but who would want to date a carbon copy of themself? In fact, I started branching out my interests and going to the movies more often because of you. I eventually started finding joy in this activity. You loved it, and I realized I also felt fulfillment in going to them. I just didn't dedicate that much effort into it before.

Just like that, it became part of the normal activities we would do together. Was that not special enough for you? There is a satisfaction you feel when you start finding pleasure in doing things your partner likes. It brings them happiness, and then it slowly but surely brings joy to you as well.

I'm not saying I would do something I hated doing just for the sake of spending time with you. I wouldn't go to a transit museum with you every week, no matter how much you adored it. That would derail my level of tolerance for that museum.

Unfortunately, these activities that I found out I enjoy give me agony; I don't know when I can do them again. They still remind me of you, and it hurts.

I'm not sure if I did too much that day, or if my eagerness to surprise you and make you happy felt overwhelming. I hope not. I hope you're out there thinking about the kiss we exchanged at the ice cream store with longing.

*Hey, I wish I could feel your soft cashmere sweater against my skin while we hug again.*

I went to a comedy/singing show with some friends today, and I couldn't help but notice that, at the table in front of us, there was a guy sitting by himself. He was wearing this brown cashmere sweater that reminded me of yours; they were practically the same color and texture.

Although I could easily tell that he wasn't you, that was the only vision my eyes wanted to see. My eyes locked in on him for a while. Looking at the sweater brought back irresistible memories. There was also the delusional hope that somehow you were sitting in front of me. I hoped that you would eventually turn around and smile upon noticing me behind you.

My brain is still trying to understand that you are gone. All it wants is to keep being delusional and to give that man a hug. It would fulfill the fantasy if he smelled just like you. Maybe he would have hugged me like you did. Maybe feeling my hands wrapped around his cashmere sweater would feel like I was touching yours once again. I was so desperate to see you again, to recreate that passion only you could make me feel. Unfortunately, that was all a dream. A dream so crushing that I should have branded it as a lucid dream, or even as a nightmare.

I reached a point where I had to excuse myself so I could go to the bathroom and sit by myself on the toilet. How picturesque . . . It was the only place where I could find some privacy. It was the only place I could curse the world I live in for not allowing me to have you. It was the only place where I was safe to let my face express my emotions without a fake smile.

You see, the thing is that weeks have gone by, and all I can still think about is you. I'm not interested in knowing your whereabouts and what you are doing. I simply think about all our moments together. How I wish I still had you in my life or that there would be a world where I could look down and see your face on my phone accompanied by a text.

All these emotions have taken over me lately, and I can't find happiness anymore. All this grief is love with nowhere to go. Unspent and unwanted. *I miss you.* That's the truth. I miss you. I miss you. I freaking miss you like crazy.

That sweater was evidence of that. How well I had gotten to know your interests and your love of that cozy vibe: pillows, a nice warm blanket, a candle, a comfy sweater, a brainless movie on the TV, and a thunderstorm outside. How I ache to be able to live that fantasy with you. How I hoped that coziness could have been our everyday life. You don't understand how my heart beats for you. How it screams your name. How it's constantly reminding me of you. How it wishes for you. It already knows you, and its only ambition is to make you the happiest version of yourself every single day for the rest of your life because it loves nothing more than seeing you smile. How it would have loved to prepare you a nice bubble bath after a hard day at work, although it knows you don't take them. There was hope that maybe you would start loving them the same way I did. In the same way that I didn't know you and, upon meeting you, I started to love you.

The hardest part about that experience was how the sight of that cashmere sweater made me think of when you called our relationship over. You had told me the news while sitting on my bed, and after that long talk, all I wanted was a hug from you. And so, you did. In fact, we cuddled for a long time. Just our bodies on my bed for one last time. You cared. I know you did.

You even shaved your beard to try to make it easier for me because you knew I liked it. You even gave me several kisses on my forehead while we cuddled, my weak spot. You wanted to make me feel better, and that was a way to do so. The dampness on your clothes that once came from me falling asleep on top of your chest with my mouth open was now because of the tears that slowly fell down my face.

At the same time, we managed to joke about the experience. I said that it felt like putting down a dog. We wanted to cherish that last hug together because we knew it would be the last one. We knew that once you left through the door, we would never see each other again. Thanks to that comparison, we were able to laugh through the pain, and in all honesty . . . that made me think even harder that I had found *the one*. That one person you can laugh with even in the most heartbreaking moments possible. How could a heartbreak feel good in a place like this? How could a heartbreak make me see that you were *the one* but, at the same time, you would walk away forever after that hug? I didn't want it to end. Why would I? The ending would symbolize that I had lost you. What I wanted was to freeze that moment for as long as I could. Just like when I had to put down my childhood dog. I knew it was the last hug, the last hoorah, and because of that, I didn't want it to perish.

I cleaned up my face and left the bathroom, ready to put on that fake smile again and sit with my friends while I tried to find pleasure in the show. While trying to avoid letting my eyes look at that cashmere sweater, and in turn, relive all that pain again.

*Hey, what am I supposed to write about when nothing bluntly reminds me of you?*

I wanted to have this passage talk about something sweet that reminded me of you and what you stood for. Instead, this is the opposite. This is about how after a long day of thinking about you, I still can't shake you from my head. It gets exhausting . . . It never stops! I can't connect you to an object when your existence is always with me.

It isn't news to me at this point, but I woke up unable to get out of bed. I tossed and turned all night long, wishing that I had you next to me under the blankets. Instead, depression was the warm body that had cuddled me to sleep the night before.

It has been so hard to find the motivation to roll out of bed and live my life. If my life is simply not worth living without you, why would I even bother? I'm usually unable to gather the courage to do so and start my day. Checking my phone to see if, by the grace of whatever entity is above us, I had received a text from you. Of course not. Do you still care about me like I care about you?

Today, I tried my best to go on about my day, and I ended up meeting some friends after work for one of those televised late-night comedy shows.

I was the first one to arrive at the set, and it was so devastating to see people walk in, two at a time, as couples. I came to realize that I was the only single person from this group. The only one who still had to figure out life alone, without having someone to hold their hand.

I wonder what they said when we all left to go home. Did they lay in bed together commenting about how I was single? About how I have been so alone lately? Maybe they didn't even pay attention to the fact that I was by myself. Maybe they don't care. Unfortunately, I do.

I don't think you understand the pain I felt when we went to a bar afterward. I felt like I was the odd man out. Everyone was in little duets around the table, and I sat on the outskirts of every single conversation, trying to jump into one.

I wish you had been there. Maybe that way I would have felt like I belonged there. I wanted you to be there with me so we could live another core memory. I didn't care if you ended up spilling your drink all over me, if you hated the night, or if you said you didn't relate to those friends that you had never met. At least I wouldn't have felt lonely. I wouldn't have felt abandoned.

On my way home after that bar, I queued this stupid sad song on Spotify. I wanted it to keep me company while I walked home after too many drinks. Stumbling and closing my eyes, here and there, because all the lyrics make me think of you.

I hate that I still miss you, and I hate myself for not being strong enough to let you go. You're almost like a piece of bubblegum stuck on my shoe. With time it starts rubbing off, but there are still pieces that will always stay there. Even if you try to scrape it off with a stick or something pointy, you can never fully get rid of it. I know this isn't the most romantic metaphor, but that's how I feel while I'm desperately trying to free my mind from your existence.

You know that feeling when you sit in a subway car and a sad song that gets to you starts playing? That feeling when you squint your eyes hard so no one can see your eyes get wet? That was me when I was on my way back home.

I thought about how alone I felt. I kept seeing other couples, and my jealousy screamed louder than any of my other thoughts. I wanted you. I wanted to be able to hold you. Instead, I was fighting my tears while the most beautiful, romantic song played in my ears. Another thing that made me think of you.

All I wanted was to turn to the girl sitting next to me and ask her if it was okay for me to rest my head on her shoulder. The sadness was too much of a burden. I wanted to ask her to put her arm around me. I wanted to ask her to be you, just for a minute. I wanted to ask her if she could say that she still believes in us and that I don't have to face life alone.

Being the single person in a group of coupled-up friends is the worst feeling there is. It accentuates the contrast between our different lives. Am I the crazy spinster in a comedy show whose job is to be the comedy relief and never find love? To be stuck in an endless string of bad dates asking themselves: *When will love show up on a Christmas morning?*

*Hey, I'm really done reminiscing about you.*

Recently, I have been stuck in a constant state where the only thing I can do is think about you. It has reached a point where it isn't healthy, and I'm sick of it.

I'm also facing writer's block, which is making me struggle to think about new stories to write about. What once came so naturally upon seeing the most mundane object is currently an active exercise. I need to think hard about what to write next. With that, I end up forcing myself to recall your existence in the hopes I get the motivation to write something.

That's the most counterproductive thing I could ever think of. Especially since I'm also trying to heal myself and detach from you. Trying to move on. However, at the same time, I'm also trying to write about you, which makes me unable to move on. What a conundrum! Maybe I should have learned more about writing before doing so as a mechanism to express my grief in a healthy way. I would probably have learned to keep it brief, in a few bullet points, like a journal instead of ending up with a book.

In fact, I often reflect on it: *What is the reason I'm even writing anymore?* I thought I had concluded that we had to heal first. I'm codependent, you're hyper-independent. My attachment style is anxious, yours is avoidant. It will fail again unless we improve ourselves. Why am I so stubborn then? This book will likely not get you back as it was all delusions in my head talking.

I need to stop writing about you because I'm not a masochist. I no longer want to relive the memories we shared by writing them down. They are constantly bringing me pain and suffering. I wonder why I'm so in love with you that I feel like the world would want to hear our beautiful story. All these questions can just be summarized in a simpler one: *Why do I get so weak at the thought of simply letting you go?*

It saddens me to think I can't write anything new about you anymore. For a second, I believe myself when my subconscious tells me we have no more memories. I already wrote about them all. In fact, we weren't strong enough to have had enough stories that could fill all the pages of a book. If our love wasn't that strong, am I a fool for still obsessing over you?

Given that it's unhealthy, I go back to the original question: *Why am I still doing this?* The answer can be boiled down to the truth. The most problematic scenario you can find.

The thought of not loving you anymore. That we weren't that strong. That someday I will be able to live my life without you just fine. The truth is that these thoughts hurt. They hurt as much as the pain I felt when I lost you. Getting over you will make me see that we weren't soulmates and that it was all but a futile crush. I refuse that world.

I'm both lost and found in this journey, constantly living between realms. When I used to see you, I saw a home. Nowadays, reminiscing about you is like adding more rooms to this shelter. When I close my eyes, I see a place where I can be myself, because I was comfortable being who I am next to you. I find myself in those dreams often. They give my life meaning. A future where we both feel lucky, unique, and special. I feel the love and happiness that irradiate through all the *what ifs* that are suddenly answered. I'm infinitely falling for this image of you.

But I'm also lost. I don't have the keys to this place. Even if I did, I lost the map that would lead me there. If I found this house by chance, maybe someone had already beat me in this race. Maybe it has already been destroyed and is currently being rebuilt to be something else.

In this journey, I spent so long chasing this imaginary home that I ended up neglecting myself and my own needs. I'm both lost and found.

Luckily for me, or maybe not, writing a book has always been on my bucket list. This made me decide to embrace the problematic truth and to try to find inspiration again.

I have been reading a few love poems to try to find comfort in the many broken hearts out there, struggling to stay cheerful through the pain. I also have been trying to watch romance movies before going to bed so I can tap into this old hopeless romantic soul in the hopes of trying to get encouragement from their stories. While I watch them, I can't help but observe something about these movies. Although you wanted to live in one of them and be the charming protagonist who has Mr. Perfect come and save them, you never noticed the most important detail in all these romances. In all of them, the main couple always fights! Shocker, right? I think you have been keeping a blind eye to this important detail because it would damage your reality, shattering your view of the perfect relationship.

All of that is really confusing to me. I know I'm being delusional by thinking that the universe is giving me a signal. That I shouldn't quit after the big fight. I simply have to overlook the big picture and let this be my time to turn a blind eye. Letting me focus on the only part I want to see, the one where I can find comfort. The part in the movie where the protagonists realize that their love ends up being stronger than their adversities. It's the drive that binds them together through their conflict. They see that they can thrive together by embracing their imperfections and who they are. They end up reuniting after that because that's love, and they love one another.

But what if I want to give up? What if I want to stop believing in a future together? Am I strong enough to do so?

So, tell me, if you would close your eyes for a second and picture love, what do you see?

*Hey, tonight was such a scary night.*

Today was the day of the weekly meet-up with my group of friends at the local gay bar. At least, it's local for them because they all live in that neighborhood. However, I live in another one, so I usually have to travel a bit to get there. I used to live in their area, and that bar became one of our weekly hangout spaces back then. Even after I left the neighborhood, we kept meeting up at our regular spot.

This week, I was desperately looking forward to it. I wanted to try to take the ever-growing pain of losing you away from me. Yet, at the same time, I was also hesitant about meeting them there.

I wanted to stop thinking about you, but I wasn't sure if a gay bar would be the best place for me to be in. I get jealous whenever I see a couple together, especially a gay one. I can't stop wishing that it was us. That it was you and I holding hands. I still miss you.

Inside the bar, we were sitting in our usual corner booth. The only one surrounded by windows, the same one you sat in when I introduced you to these friends.

It was a regular night, and after long hours of chatting with my friends, it was time to leave. It was starting to get late, and I still had a long ride back home. As I was getting ready to call it a night, one of my friends decided that he wanted to partake in a round of flip cup that was about to happen. Just a fun way to end the night—it wasn't a college bar!

Although I wasn't going to play, I decided to stick around a little longer to cheer for him. It was a normal thing in our group. While we were waiting for it to start, I noticed that my friend kept looking through my shoulder as we were talking. He was unable to keep eye contact with me as if he was hypnotized. I sensed that something was off, and I was intrigued by his strange behavior. The only way to figure out what was happening was by following his stare. It led me to look through the window into the street.

To my surprise, there was a big splash of blood on the concrete pavement and a broken beer bottle. I was shocked! I had no idea what had just happened two feet next to me through the other side of the wall. Panic ran through my veins with a side of fear. I thought about how I was supposed to head out five minutes earlier. I could have been there for that! But most importantly, one unanswered question remained: *Why was there so much blood on the street?*

I assumed it wasn't a hate crime and that we weren't in danger of being under attack at that gay bar since nothing else terrifying was happening. Unfortunately, this is a common fear for many people when violence against the community seems to be a common headline.

I was confused and alone. There was this sadness overcoming my emotional state. I could only think that if it had been me, I wouldn't have you to help me. Even though I had my friends there to aid me if that scenario had happened, I couldn't deny that I still felt isolated. At the end of the night, they would walk home on their own paths, and I would have to go home by myself since I'm the only one who doesn't live in that neighborhood. What if something happened to me along the road when I was alone and vulnerable?

Later on, I found out it wasn't a hate crime but a robbery instead. One of the regulars at the bar saw it and stepped in to help, but he got hit in the face with a beer bottle. I won't say his name, but you know who he is. When you were there, I introduced you to the crowd. That group of people had become a community I saw frequently, so it felt right to integrate you.

In a turn of events, the boyfriend of the person who got hit with the bottle was fuming. He wasn't mad at the situation but at how reckless his partner had been. The reasoning was that the robber could have had a hidden knife or maybe a gun. His boyfriend should have called for help at the bar instead of risking his life.

I tried calming him down and asked him not to blame his partner. In the heat of the moment, he had tried his best to do the right thing. He tried to help.

Unfortunately, it was to no avail. He was so scared, angry,

and pissed off at the thought of something worse happening to his boyfriend.

When I heard the discussion that was slowly starting to happen between the couple, I was also angry. Not at the partner but at the words being used. I wanted them to respect each other, to understand that love is such a beautiful thing, and that they should not shame one another for doing what they think is right. You should protect love instead of trying to find arguments when people are acting from the kindness of their hearts. I was also jealous that they had one another.

I couldn't take it anymore at that point. I was overwhelmed with emotions, and it was my time to go. I used that moment as an opportunity to leave the bar and head home. I was sad, nervous, afraid, jealous, and conflicted. I wanted everyone to cherish their loved ones while they were still around, but I couldn't.

Outside, I looked at the pool of blood next to the entrance and paid attention to the many cops that had appeared on the scene to investigate the situation. Who knew the dangers that might appear during my journey home? I was alone, and the robber was still on the loose. If something happened to me as well, I wonder if you would notice or even care. That situation forced me to stop in my tracks and made me think about a big existential question: *Why do I have to be alone against the constant struggles that exist in this world?*

Why aren't you by my side? Hanging out with my friends and acting as a strong couple? If there is strength in numbers, at the end of the day, I'm the weakest of my peers. One is the smallest number; it will always lose.

I have always had to rely on myself since I was a child, a time when I had to hide who I was and my sexuality because I was too scared of my parents kicking me out of my house. At the same time, I was also unable to relate to my classmates in the small town I grew up in, which led me to only have virtual friends. Until the day I left for college in a bigger town. That was where I found my people and started to be able to express my sexuality and myself. Freely.

I have never been able to rely on my parents to satisfy my needs. They always rejected my negative feelings since it meant that they were failing at parenting. If I felt off, it would imply they were inadequate to do their number one responsibility, to nurture and provide. If I felt cold, I would hear that it wasn't cold. I also couldn't feel sadness or be depressed. I had to be constantly happy for them to feel accomplished with their parenting skills. Even when it came to my grandmother dying, my dad couldn't gather the courage to tell me what had happened when he was trying to introduce me to the concept of death. He was too afraid I would be sad. The result was a scarred child who, up to this day, is unable to deal with the concept of death.

Later in life, when I moved to New York City, fresh out of college, I had to rely on myself to survive, pay the bills, make friends, find a job in my professional field, and even juggle immigration services. A choice I made because I wanted to be able to live in a country where I would have more rights—mainly to be able to adopt a child down the line.

In all honesty, all of these frustrations were starting to come crashing down. Those hard-hitting questions just slapped me in the face, one after the other, and each one overwhelmed me more than the previous one. How much longer will I be able to survive on my own? Why do I even have to be on my own? Why do I need to be stuck with my own pain, day after day? Why is there no one else to support me? Do I need another person for that, or will I ever be pleased with myself? Why do I need someone so badly? If I have been alone most of my life, why am I so desperate to have someone by my side now?

As I walked down the road that would lead me home, I realized that I had to learn again to survive on my own. If I keep looking behind me, at the memories of when we were together, I will miss the turn that I need to take that's right ahead of me.

*Hey, today I forced myself to go on a date . . . what a terrible idea it was.*

Remember when I said I'm the world's most terrible liar? That hasn't changed. I have been feeling so lonely lately that I broke the vow not to get back into dating.

I'm still trying to figure myself out and come to an understanding of my codependent tendencies. Yes, *tendencies*, not codependency. I recently started seeing a therapist, and he wants me to start changing the way I view the world.

These tendencies were yelling at me to get back into the dating scene because I don't want to be alone. I'm never happy by myself. The truth is that I wasn't ready to go on a date. I still needed more time to mourn your loss and to learn to control this way of dealing with relationships—a tool not to be by myself.

On the other hand, my internal needs didn't want to spend one more night alone, so it was back to the dating apps for me. By the way, I'm still using my old profile. I haven't deleted it and started a new one. Now, the reason isn't because I'm talking to you but because our match is still there, and I enjoy looking at it.

I matched with this one person who, after a quick chat, invited me out on a date. As the day approached, I started to realize the error I had made. I didn't feel any desire to go on a date just for the sake of going on a date. I even considered canceling it, the day before, as my anxiety grew stronger. My mind, however, told me he was a person with real feelings and that it would probably hurt his ego. Especially since he had been the one inviting me. I recalled how my ego felt when someone canceled a date at the last minute, followed by them saying they weren't ready. It made me feel miserable. With that in mind, I forced myself to do it. No bad could come from it because I was already living with the worst outcome: missing you.

Since I was working remotely that day, I went to a coffee shop to do some work in the afternoon. We had agreed that he would meet me there later when his schedule was free. As the time for his arrival approached, I realized I had picked the worst possible place for a date. It was too silent, and not a single conversation could be heard. I didn't want to be that person who disturbs other people while they are busy on their laptops, so I had to think of a change of plans. If this were anything like our first date, our laughter would soon fill that room. Maybe we would even be kicked out of there.

An indecisive person having to make last-minute changes to the plans? Why? When he arrived, I provided him with an alternative, to go for a walk while I finished my coffee. That way, we would be able to talk in peace without being judged for being too loud. He just needed to buy something for the walk to keep me company. When his turn came to order something at the counter, he chose to buy . . . a cookie?

My face was in disbelief. A coffee shop had been his idea! Yet, he picked the opposite option? It wasn't quirky; it was just plain weird. Preferring your coffee in the form of a cookie didn't have the same ring to it as taking it lukewarm—strike one. At least he was attractive when I met him in person.

We left the coffee shop and started walking aimlessly. Luckily, we were able to pick up topics of conversation, which was a big positive, but on the other hand, there was little chemistry. Unluckily, he wasn't you, and I wasn't reliving the day I met you. Things were so different this time. Even the conversations we were having were so mundane that they highlighted the contrast from our first date even more.

Shortly after meeting you, we were already telling each other stories about our families. Especially about our mothers and our childhood memories. I still remember when you told me, on our first date, a story about a trip to a McDonald's in Paris with your family. We were able to hit it off from the start as if we already knew one another from a past life. In comparison, I had to answer all the basic date questions today. The classic "How many siblings do you have?" followed by the mandatory "How often do you go home to see your family?"

Deep inside, that interaction made me feel uncomfortable as I kept asking myself how many more times these questions would come up on dates. The thought of me answering them over and over again to different people was too much for me at the moment. I'm worried that, at some point, I will become robotic when providing answers, detaching myself from any meaningful connection a date with a new person can bring. Eventually, I'll lose all the hope a first date usually comes with. I will ask myself why I'm even doing that when you already know the answer to those questions he asked. You even know the names of my siblings, their love lives, our relationship, their struggles, and their upbringings. Yet, to this stranger, I had to start anew.

I couldn't help but think that this scenario will repeat itself, and I will soon begin an endless loop of first dates that go nowhere. When in reality, the only loop I wanted to be stuck in was with you. Kissing you over and over and over and over and over again. *Your* lips, not his. There was no chemistry between me and him.

Coincidentally, the two of us were walking the same street as our first date, and it was also cold that afternoon. Although this time I had a cozy jacket on, I was still feeling chilly. That led me to mention that I'm always cold, and upon hearing that, he continued keeping his distance from me while we walked without direction. Wow! That interaction made me lose part of the hope that things could potentially work out with him. Back then, you had the opposite reaction. You used it as a way to lay your arm around me to heat me up and even offered me your beanie. I wish I had taken you up on your offer back then. If I had kept it, at least, I would have something that smelled like you on cold nights when I lay in bed alone.

The cherry on top of the date was when he said he wanted to go somewhere warm. Finally!

After rejecting my suggestion, he opened his phone to look at other places in the area. That was when he realized the arcade bar we had visited was in the area. He was set on going there, like you were. That was the cue for the panic to settle in. I didn't want to ruin the place where I shared so many special memories with you. That passionate first kiss, remember? What if this guy kissed me there as well, and destroyed that experience with the lack of sparks between us?

Inside the bar, there was no one. It was truly empty. This time we had space around us because we had gone there too early on a workday, not because people were avoiding us, walking away from that annoying couple that no one wants to get close to as they keep kissing in the middle of the bar.

He decided to sit at the counter to keep the banter going. My mind was numb at that point. Why did he decide to go to an arcade to talk, especially when there were prettier bars around us? An arcade isn't a random place to simply go sit at the bar. You decide to go to one with your date to assess the intimacy. The other person's smile while they watch you play. The little hip push when you play a two-player game, so they can throw you off. You want to experience that laugh. Most importantly, you want to experience that kiss after a game is over.

There was only one thing that could save me. Crosswords!

So, I tried mimicking our second date to see how well we bounced ideas off one another. Sadly, that didn't solve anything.

It didn't take us long to decide to call it a day and leave the bar. Once outside, there was this awkward stare that couldn't be read. It could either be someone wanting a goodbye kiss or what he ended up saying, "I didn't feel a romantic connection, only friend vibes."

"No judgments, the feeling is mutual," was my response.

After parting ways, I wondered how many times this story would repeat itself. More precisely, why did it have to repeat when I had already found you? You know my story, I know yours, and we were so good for one another. Why do I have to lose my time in this hellhole that dating can be? Maybe I should have listened to myself when I thought I wasn't ready for this date. That I shouldn't date just to avoid being alone.

I really need to start loving myself.

*Hey, I have been trying to plan a solo trip to fight my code-pendent tendencies.*

I'm starting to get fed up with them. They prevent me from being comfortable when I'm by myself. My thoughts are constantly screaming at me to go back into dating so I don't feel so lonely, and I have to do something to fight them.

That's why I'm looking at getting away for a while so I can learn how to be content with being single. Annoyingly, I'm reminded of my Christmas break after meeting you. During that trip, I flew solo to Austria because I needed an escape from being with my parents for two weeks in Portugal.

I was anxious, I'm not going to lie. Especially because I'm one of those people who hates doing things by themselves. A single ticket to the movie theater is enough to send me down a spiral of loneliness and despair. In fact, I had tried solo traveling in college, and I only survived one day in Dublin before I reached my breaking point. I ended up finding someone to explore the city with me on my second day. I wanted to share that experience with someone else!

To me, that's what makes traveling so beautiful. When it's a collection of shared memories, they aren't only yours. If something would happen to one person, at least there would be another one who would carry that legacy.

Last Christmas, I tried to embrace my fears of solo traveling as I thought they would overcompensate the other option—being alone with my parents for two weeks. With that frame of mind, I gathered the courage to embark on that journey to Austria.

I did enjoy being there and walking at my own pace, only seeing what I wanted to see and skipping what I had no desire to explore. For instance, I thought, "If I don't go to the Museum of Modern Art in New York, why would I go to the one in Vienna?" Fortunately, I had no one with me who would reject this thought and say they wanted to visit it. I didn't have to compromise!

However, I also saw the most beautiful and romantic sceneries, and all that I wished for, at those moments, was for you to be there next to me. In fact, I saw so many beautiful Christmas markets that I wanted you to experience alongside me. It was weird how I was living the most thrilling experience without the person who loved this season the most.

I would find a Christmas tree everywhere I walked, hidden somewhere: on a patio of a house, on a corner, on a dead end, simply everywhere! With each one I would run into, I would think of how much I would have loved to embark on this scavenger hunt with you. Trying to find as many of them as possible because they brought you joy. Giving another meaning to the emoji that was once next to your name on my phone.

Somehow, I was able to find an experience that would top all those desires. I was in the biggest Christmas market, out of the many that Vienna had to offer, and this one had an open plaza with little stores surrounding a fountain that branched out into smaller paths. Up north stood a string quartet on the roof of a store in front of the biggest Christmas tree I had seen. It would've felt like a movie if it had been snowing. Like one of those lame Hallmark movies. One of those movies that end with the most romantic kiss under that giant tree.

As an alternative, I thought of us and that maybe you could spend Christmas with me one year. We could do a little trip like that one and explore new ways to celebrate your favorite time of the year.

Suddenly, I saw something that woke me up from that daydream. Everyone was looking up and quickly taking their phones to start recording something. I was as confused as a deer in headlights, but I understood that I was also supposed to look up.

I couldn't believe my own eyes. This giant bright red heart was traveling across the plaza on a zip line. I couldn't understand what it was made of. I could only see it shine and illuminate the plaza. It traveled very slowly, but it didn't prevent it from being captivating. It was a majestic presence that I couldn't take my eyes out of. It was mesmerizing! Just like us, traveling slowly with time.

I took it as a metaphor. I shouldn't rush things with you because no matter how fast we traveled, I knew the result would be beautiful. I realized I was right to think that way when that heart came to a halt after it reached a big dark tree.

Then pure magic happened. A million smaller hearts that sat on the branches of that tree slowly started to illuminate. What once was a dark tree, covered in shadows, was now the most beautifully illuminated tree with many smaller hearts spreading through every branch. They gave it life, color, and meaning. It gave the tree a reason to live again.

It was one of the most romantic sights I had ever seen. However, it was a memory that was destined to only be mine. I still wish you had been there, though. I wanted to see if your eyes would have teared up slightly. I wonder if I would have told you it was like a metaphor for when you walked into my life and brightened it. I know you love those words of affirmation.

Thankfully, we texted endless messages whenever I got back to my Airbnb and got one of the greatest pleasures of modern society: Wi-Fi. In those moments, I felt less alone.

At first, I thought I was being boring by sending you too many pictures, but you were fast to reject that idea. You told me you wanted to keep seeing photos of my trip to keep living that experience through me.

Somehow, it was like you were there with me in spirit. The memories that were once mine slowly started to become shared as I kept telling you everything I had seen. I would go to bed every night with a six-hour time zone difference without feeling alone in that cold apartment. You were there with me via text, warming my heart and my cold bed. Making me wish for the moment I would return to New York so I could hug you again. Making me wonder when we could go on a short trip together.

If a solo trip could feel this magical, the thought of what we could create together was a delightful treat to my imagination.

Today, I'm looking at flights for a little getaway to recenter myself. To learn how to be comfortable when I'm alone and to see if I can stop dreaming about you. This time, I'm going solo, not to run away from my parents but to try to feel independent. I wonder if I will be able to have fun without having you to text at the end of the day. I wish it didn't have to be this hard.

I don't want to travel to run away from anybody or anything. I want to travel because it's a beautiful thing. Just like you. I want to travel so that one day, twenty years from now, I can talk about the time I was in a foreign country with the man of my life, and we shared the most beautiful moments. Those shared memories. Romantic stories that will always be ours. Locked in our hearts. Forever. Until we die.

# Step Five:

# Acceptance

Day Thirty-Eight

*Hey, today I finished the last mini Diet Coke that was in my fridge.*

It had been there, waiting eagerly for you, for a while. The sole reason for those sodas being in my fridge was because I had bought them for you. After all, we did match on Hinge because you said you were obsessed with Diet Coke, and I promptly asked you how many cans you had in your apartment. Later on, I even went to the extreme of buying you a very special Christmas ornament: a small bedazzled can of Diet Coke. I gave it to you the day before I left to go home for the holidays.

Knowing that I always tried to please you, the first time you came to my apartment, I was able to say that I had six cans of this beverage on my fridge. I opted to get mini cans so it wouldn't feel like a big commitment to drink them. That way, in the morning, you could choose to drink lukewarm coffee, orange juice, or a Diet Coke while having breakfast.

Because of my parents' relationship with food, cooking wasn't the activity I found the most comfort and passion in. In fact, I would rather do the dishes. But, somehow, I enjoyed preparing you breakfast every time you came over. You were so busy with work that I wanted to make sure you were as stress-free as possible so you could focus your energy on spending time with me. Even though I felt like the center of my parents' fights always happened around a meal, it was the opposite with you. I saw your happiness when I prepared a vegetarian feast for you. That made me realize I had to start changing my views toward cooking and food. By shutting down my childhood trauma, I was able to find pleasure in the activity I once hated. All because of the happiness I saw on your face.

I wanted you to associate the days spent at my apartment with pleasure. For you to look forward to coming back to my apartment because you knew I would take care of you. Your happiness was my driver in life. Seeing you smile was like looking at a constellation meant just for me.

I would usually offer you a Diet Coke before you headed out so you could have something to distract you on the long commute back to your place. It was almost like I had every detail of the day planned to ensure you valued every second we got to spend together, in the comfort of my apartment.

Close your eyes and think of the sound of a tab opening a can. Imagine the sound of ice clinking on a glass followed by a fizzling sound as a carbonated drink is poured over ice cubes. What do you think of?

Most often than not, you associate those audible experiences with Coca-Cola. It's all thanks to their impressive marketing strategy and how well they execute it. On the other end of the spectrum, I wish I had nailed that strategy. I craved that if you would close your eyes and think of happiness, you would think of me. That the image etched in your mind would be of waking up in my bed before heading toward my living room for a nice breakfast. Ready to relax on my couch while wearing your least favorite type of pajamas, clothes in general. I have a roommate, and I didn't want him to catch you lying on my couch like a French girl.

I wish that was your train of thought when you envisioned happiness.

To me, nothing is sweeter than feeling comfortable with someone in the waking hours of the morning. When you're still trying to wake up, feeling the most vulnerable, not fully operational yet. But you still feel relaxed and comfortable next to someone. While you're in your pajamas, with messy hair, bloodshot eyes, and a sense of confusion in your stare.

Nonetheless, seeing that smile next to me in bed was the boost I needed to get up and start the day. It didn't matter if the person that I fell asleep next to turned out to be the complete opposite of the one I saw in the morning. All I knew was that I wanted it in my life. That was why I started to fall in love with you. You didn't make my mornings just feel less lonely. You complemented them. Even if it meant waking up earlier than you to brew your lukewarm coffee. You would give me a reason to smile as soon as I left my bed instead of me trying to find it somewhere else. I was ready to tackle the day.

I guess that at the end of it all, those actions and thoughts are the codependent tendencies that are still around me. I put so much effort into your happiness since it provided me joy that I wonder if I lost my sense of purpose. My mission in life was to make you happy. Just like my mother, I needed that in my life to feel fulfilled and content with myself.

Part of me blames myself as I know, in retrospect, that I should have just let it flow naturally and not tried so hard. That eagerness to make you smile and solve all your problems was what caused you to feel smothered. I still need to spend more time learning more about myself. There is a line between being a nice person and being codependent, trying to fix everyone. A line that I still can't draw.

All I know today is that I need to stop thinking about these things; it won't change the outcome. Blaming myself for buying the Diet Cokes or that Christmas ornament too soon won't bring you back. All I can do is try to focus on the future. Making sure I learn, so I can be a better lover in the future.

All of these memories need to be left in the past. Alongside all those cans I got you that no longer take up space in my apartment. Out of sight, out of mind.

*Hey, this healing journey has been making me constantly think about you, and I'm done.*

Although I have my doubts, there is hope in me that the common saying "you attract what you are" isn't true. We both had broken hearts when we met, and I ask myself if our chemistry was simply a product of that pain. While I try to fix mine, I can't help but wonder if you're trying to fix yours as well. At least that was the excuse you used to cut me out of your life. I genuinely believed you. You told me then that you had to be selfish and put yourself first because you still had to figure yourself out. You still carry trauma from your past with you, and you need to heal from it to fully thrive in a relationship.

In my ideal and impossible scenario, we both would be working on our issues and fixing our problems, returning to one another stronger than ever in the future. This can be a bit contradictory to what I believe in, but I can't change the cards that have been dealt. I firmly believe that relationships don't need to end for people to repair themselves. I believe that relationships simply need to hold a safe space for people to heal and grow together.

This way of viewing the world comes from the fact that we will never be the same people we are today. We develop ourselves over time. A five-year relationship won't feature the same people that once existed at the beginning of their story. They also won't be the same in ten years. With time, people change, but their core values will remain the same. It will highlight the most beautiful thing, which is mutual respect. Love is a choice we make to let people grow and heal at their own pace and to still be there for them no matter what. We see and believe in their potential.

However, at the moment, I can't grow with you, and I need to realize that you are no longer here.

With time, I have also understood I can't change people or ask them to change themselves for me. I learned this lesson the hard way when substance abuse tore apart my previous relationship. I couldn't make him stop his self-destructive addiction for me because, without me, there was no reason not to go back to it. He had to do it for himself, whenever he was ready for it.

In the same way, I can't make you change or heal your broken heart. I can give you a shoulder to cry on when things are rough. I can give you the most unconditional love and support you have ever experienced. I can be your personal emotional support human.

But I can't be your savior. I can't convince you that you're worth fighting for and worthy of love. I can't convince you that I will never give up on you. I can't convince you that I won't run away or try to hurt you. I know you're still afraid of being hurt again. I can prove that I was ready to fight for you until my spirits are worn out from endless rejections. But I can't make you understand that I meant what I said: *Forever is until we find out if the afterlife will provide us with another reality where we can still be together.*

I could have given you all the proof you wanted, but if you never convince yourself that you have to change the ways you love—if you never do it for yourself, to be a better lover in the future—then there will never be hope for us, no matter how hard I try. Loving is also letting go.

Losing you made me realize that I had to heal. Mainly around my codependent tendencies. That's why I started doing so; I have been reading and going to therapy. More importantly, I have been doing it for myself. I want to be a better partner in future relationships.

Although I still wish it was with you, I can't force it onto you if you aren't ready to heal. I must move on.

I might have started this book on the opposite note. I was desperate to get you back, only to come to the realization that it was worthless. Loving a heart that isn't ready to be loved is the first step to losing your own. It looks like this whole Mo Melo pseudonym was a demented dream where I would win you back, even though you told me you weren't ready for it. Doing so would result in the same ending if you aren't ready to start your healing journey.

I put a lot of thinking into flipping things around and signing this book with my real name instead. However, I realized that I have written a lot of personal things about you, and I want to respect your privacy. I still care about you. I will never stop caring about you.

There are many thoughts that lead me to stand in the middle of this emotional intersection. On one hand, I can heal and move on. Hopefully, I can find someone new. When I'm ready. On the other hand, I can keep working on improving myself and not lose hope that you're doing the same. Just for us to be reunited, stronger than ever, in the future. Unfortunately, this last option would require me to wait, and I'm an impatient person.

I assume it's worth waiting for the things we believe in. The same way you wait impatiently every year for Christmas to come so you can decorate your apartment, put on those cozy sweaters, and be immersed in a parade of colorful flashing lights, I could wait for you.

Will you think I'm crazy if I say that, at the moment, I'm comfortable not knowing? I will wait happily, even though I'm not sure if this is the right choice. I need to learn to embrace the uncertainty. Today's confusion will be the much-needed reassurance to future me. I will no longer lose time thinking about *what ifs* a few years down the line. I will know for a fact that I tried my best and it either worked out or not. I won't daydream about the possibility of you being the one that got away because I didn't wait.

I will be able to say, with certainty, that if you were the one, things would have worked out. I had given you your space, and you knew that my door was constantly open for a new beginning. Yet, you chose not to go down that path. For that reason, I will choose to go in the opposite direction.

But to reach this level of certainty, I need to give it some time. I need to learn how to sit quietly and be comfortable not knowing until I know.

I can do that if it's love. Maybe in the future, these opposite paths will turn out to be a roundabout.

Sadly, love isn't a metaphor. Love is a decision you make every day, just like the choice you have to make to start healing your damaged heart. Your healing journey staying stagnant will only hold me back. Although I have always struggled to say no, I need to see that love is also dropping off our baggage so we travel down our path faster—in this case, your existence. Love is also letting go.

*Hey, have you seen that a new Gremlins miniseries is going to premiere soon?*

AHHHHHHHHHHHHHHHHHHHHHHHHHHHH, there, I let it out of my chest.

Interestingly, when writing that string of characters, you can't tell if that's excitement, anger, or panic. Sorry to disappoint, but it's all three.

*Gremlins* will forever be a soft spot for me. They will remind me of us watching the first movie during Christmas to cross one item from my "America Assimilation list." It was a piece of paper with several movies I had to watch for my friends to consider me American. I had created it after many friends told me, *"Never Been Kissed?* You have never seen it?" or "How about *A League of Their Own?* No? Please tell me you have at least seen *Heathers!"*

We had made that list a dear prize, something that I dug out of a drawer after realizing that picking a movie never came easy to us. The only thing we knew for sure was that watching a movie together was a better idea than watching a series. Given your busy schedule, we would probably never finish a multi-season TV show.

*Gremlins* happened to be on that list, so when a movie theater aired it, in preparation for the Christmas season, we decided we had to see it. The classic holiday comedy, *Gremlins*! Not *Home Alone*.

In true fashion of going to a movie theater, you even snuck in some candy. Not just any candy, though! It was the quirkiest Sour Patch Kids one could think of. It was a unique package designed for the number one fan of this holiday. It was a special edition box full of sour coal. Yes! The thing that naughty boys get on Christmas. It was the only time I said thank you for being on Santa's naughty list, as it got me a very special present.

Before going to the movies, you asked me what my favorite candy was, without me knowing that you intended to buy it in preparation for that night. I gave you a list of the varieties that I liked and disliked, a list that should have been very short for someone who says they like everything and are indecisive.

"I love every type of chocolate, especially the ones with peanut butter. But no liquor or caramel, and absolutely no mint chocolate. I also love gummies, but not the ones that get stuck in your teeth, like Swedish Fish. I love the sour stuff, the sugary and acidic ones!"

I soon realized that it said a lot and nothing at the same time, so I decided to Google some pictures to help you visualize my taste. That was when I saw a photo of what I assumed was a joke, something so crazy that it had to be fake: Sour Patch Kids Coal. I quickly sent it to you and said with sarcasm, "These, these are my favorite!"

Never would I have thought that you would find them and buy me several boxes. Especially because I didn't know they existed! My face of excitement and shock—when you opened your bag to give them to me—was out of this world.

Thinking about it still makes me laugh. It had been such a cool gift that I saved some of those boxes and took them with me when I went back home for Christmas. I had a spare gift as you had taught me so well.

Those gummies weren't the only thing I enjoyed. Besides your company, we loved the absurdity of that movie. It provided us with so many laughs that we rented the second one on one of the nights I spent at your apartment. That was the night you fell asleep on my chest and told me how magical that experience had been for you. To feel comfortable falling asleep next to me after a long day at work.

Today, I see that *Gremlins* are going to launch a miniseries very soon, and it's hard to picture the excitement we could have experienced when we watched it for the first time. What is even harder is the ability to tell myself that I don't need you to watch it. In fact, I can watch it without you and have a good time.

I need to accept that things can hurt, memories can hurt, but they can't define me. I need to be able to pull the reins of my own decisions and tell myself that I can do it. I might be moved by emotions and *what ifs*, but life goes on. Every lover will leave a mark on you, and after a while, you forget about it. I didn't destroy the rug that's in my living room because I got it with my ex. It's still there, and it no longer hurts me. If I detached once, I can do it again!

It's either that or I will be a mess every Christmas, and my friends can't deal any longer with me being unhinged and unwell for extended periods of time. Trust me. I can already picture their faces when I tell them I wrote a book and need their help reading it. I think all of us can fear a future where I'm that person that makes achieving a goal their entire personality trait.

As my therapist tells me, I need to reframe my mind. I need to be able to live with uncomfortable feelings and cope with them in a healthy way. I need to tell myself that I'm not my mother; I'm someone who won't seek happiness in other people. I can provide that for myself, and I'm most certainly worthy of love. I will be able to find someone who treats me well if I believe I deserve love and reject breadcrumbs.

If I was already a Gizmo in a sea of gremlins when I was a codependent mess, imagine what a healed version of myself would be like! Probably an unbearable human being who won't shut up about how healing from their codependent tendencies made them a better person or will keep going on about how putting slices of cucumber in their water made them grow three inches taller.

*Hey, I did it! I just came back from that solo trip I was planning before.*

I can't believe that what can be such a trivial thing to so many people can be such a big milestone for others. It took so much in me to finally book that trip. Deep inside me, I kept waiting for someone to join me in that adventure. I was looking for an excuse to go, someone who would pull the trigger to my desires. Someone who would validate my ideas and keep me company.

At the end of the day, I had to force myself to live my life and not wait around for anyone else. Only I can enjoy it and make myself happy.

But I can't deny it, this isn't an easy feat for me, and it also won't solve all my problems. But it's definitely a start in this new journey where I try to fight my codependent tendencies and be content alone.

Do you remember the map I have at home above my desk? That scratch-off map of the states I have been to? I still recall how we used to compare states we had been to and plan road trips across the ones I still wished to visit. Well . . . I used this trip to knock out two states from this imaginary vacation that will never happen now that you are gone. I felt the need to go explore a new city, an unfamiliar destination, so I could prove to myself that I didn't need you or anyone else to do so. I wanted to prove to myself that I can survive on my own!

I started this trip with a twenty-four-hour stay in St. Louis before hitting a city that would have been very dear to the two of us, Chicago. I decided to start this trip in St. Louis not only because I had no idea if I would ever have another excuse to scratch off Missouri from my list. But also because I met this couple from there last Christmas when I was in Austria. That way, I would be able to grab a drink or a meal with them, avoiding feeling alone on the trip.

Even though I'm still learning how to fight my codependent tendencies, I haven't mastered the art of shaking off the thought that I need people to feel complete yet. Baby steps. I'm learning to embrace that people grow at their own pace. I only hope that you aren't standing still on your journey. That you're trying to control your avoidant tendencies, so you can also have more meaningful relationships with whomever the future has in store for you. You can also see that I haven't mastered the art of detaching myself from you either.

Upon landing in St. Louis, I decided to take their subway system to save forty dollars on an Uber ride. This is when I thought that maybe I needed someone else to travel with me so we could bounce ideas off each other. We could discuss that maybe an Uber would be worth it and that I shouldn't trust my judgment. It's definitely hard to learn to care for your own needs when the universe is telling you that you need someone else to help you in the battle.

I express that because the subway that I took had cameras everywhere. It also had a TV that showed what was going on throughout the rest of the car, Big Brother in a prison type of energy. I told myself that it would actually be beneficial because I could stay alert without acting too suspicious or nervous. Luckily, their security system works very well because it was put into use shortly after I sat down.

Four security guards came in to kick some people out before a fight broke loose. Thankfully, it didn't get too violent since security called it off before the first punch was thrown. But that interaction was enough to make me panic on the inside, especially as my friends warned me that I was going to two murder capitals of the US. With that in mind, why did I decide to risk it and take public transportation?

After that dramatic scene, I arrived at my destination, ready to start walking to the restaurant I had planned to have dinner. My settings were on high alert mode, keeping an eye on my surroundings. That was how I spotted a red car driving toward me that started to slow down before passing by me. When it reached me, I saw a male driver looking at me, right in my face. Before I knew it, he was doing a U-Turn. My legs turned on their turbo mode, walking as fast as possible. I was scared. As I was about to dash to another street at the intersection, the driver called out my name.

I realized it was one of the people from the couple who

had decided to surprise me. Although we had originally made lunch plans for the next day, they had some last-minute changes of plans and were busy the next day, so he decided to surprise me upon my arrival. He knew where I was going to have dinner and which subway stop I was leaving.

When I hopped into his car, my heart was racing, and I had to stop for a minute to catch my breath; hoping there would be no more scares like that one.

The time we shared was pleasant, I have to say that. We were able to grab dinner and catch up on our lives. When we were done, he drove me to my hotel, and upon reaching my room, I started feeling feverish. Of course. Why do we either get sick on the first or last day of our trips?

I was shaking, I felt cold no matter how warm the room's thermostat claimed it was. That was when I started to wish someone was there with me to go buy some Tylenol or something else. What if I needed help, and there was no one else besides me? That realization alone made me regret having gone on a trip by myself in the first place. Can humans survive without any help? The answer is yes, but not without complaining a lot. I was able to put on some clothes and go buy Tylenol while cursing the world.

I headed back to my hotel room; 911, a number I will never forget. I don't know if you would have appreciated the joke or if you would have thought that it was too dark and insensitive for me to make. I was left to wonder if we would have fought about it or laughed. I tried my hardest to find peace in not knowing the answer. I was fighting my own demons, not imaginary *what ifs* from a relationship that no longer exists.

The next morning, after taking some more medicine, I left to explore the city. Later that day, I took a train to Chicago, which was another brilliant idea I had when planning this trip.

My thinking was that a five-hour train ride would allow me to see the landscape connecting the two cities. Perhaps if I had traveled with someone, especially a person who had grown up in the US, they would have told me that this was a weird idea. There would be nothing to see, particularly at night. I wouldn't be able to see a single tree when it was pitch dark outside. They would have probably advised me to take a plane instead or I would end up looking at my own reflection for five long hours.

In fact, it ended up being seven hours; the train came to a halt due to some construction happening on the rail system. At that point, I could no longer read *Codependent No More*, so I decided to take a nap. A plan that was interrupted by a small cockroach prancing on the seat next to mine, crawling toward me. I jumped on my seat and kicked it far away. Overall, I felt disgusted by the situation and my choices.

That's why I say that it's hard to fight my codependent tendencies. The more mistakes I made, the more I wished I had someone next to me to guide me through life. But, at the end of the day, I do need to make these mistakes because that's how I learn. Trial and error.

So, although I regretted all the terrible decisions I made, I can embrace them. They inspired me to call an Uber, instead of taking the subway at one thirty in the morning, when I got to Chicago. I was able to learn from my errors! All the pain can be worth it at the end of the day if we use it as fuel to improve ourselves.

Chicago treated me better, though! I had wanted to visit the Windy City for quite some time. It took me a long time to do it because I never had an excuse to. By excuse, I mean that I had been waiting for someone to come with me, so I could have some company. All my friends kept telling me that I would love it there, so much that I would even think about moving there. The city and the people resonated with my persona. In all honesty, the cold winter months alone are enough of a reason to make me run away from that thought, no matter how much in love with the city I would become. You, of course, already know this because it only took you one date with me to see how much I hate the cold. That was the biggest reason why I wanted to visit.

The other one was the fact that I wanted to see the city where our favorite show, *Happy Endings,* took place. I wanted to see if, by going there, I would understand some scenes and references a little bit better, enhancing the experience of re-watching some episodes.

The first day in Chicago was the hardest, I will admit it. Apparently, Chicago loves Christmas as well! It was spring and their Christmas decorations were still up! Some houses had bushes on the outside decorated like small Christmas trees, there were mistletoe ornaments in public planters, bars with

Christmas lights . . . I get it, I think that I will never look at the season the same way as before. The goal now is to be comfortable with your memory without the pain of it. But it's a hard thing to do, detaching the love and pain from thoughts that still come around so often.

I decided to do one architectural tour on my first day, as I love skyscrapers and architecture. I constantly imagined you there walking around with me, learning about the city and its buildings. I also imagined you looking at the trains above ground, admiring them for all their glory while they circled the downtown area. If you had been there, most likely, I would have looked online to see if there was a Chicago Transit Museum.

At some point during that tour, the guide led the group away from the streets and into some enigmatic buildings to explore inside. One of them included a store that sold something very emblematic of the city of Chicago: a green box with *Frango* written across the front and filled with mint chocolates.

The tour guide bought one box and passed it around for us to try. If you still remember me and all our memories, you probably can understand why this was a conundrum when it got to my hands.

Even though I hate that type of candy, I like to try new things. For me, mint chocolates were reserved for people who like to swallow their toothpaste after brushing their teeth. It isn't a flavor profile that makes me feel at ease. It makes me feel like I'm doing chores, like brushing my teeth.

That's why, when I opened your freezer, I was shocked to only see mint chocolate chip ice cream, and without second thoughts, I said that it was my least favorite ice cream flavor *ever*. I can't even say it's my least favorite because the word favorite implies associations with positive things. It's the most disgusting flavor of ice cream. Period. Weirdly enough, after slandering this sweet treat, I still wanted to try it anyway because I won't know if that one might be different.

Same thing for pickles. We joked that the best couples are the ones where one person hates pickles and the other one loves them. The latter will always get double pickles with every meal.

We were this couple, except for the "best" part of it and the fact that you would always get my pickles with one bite missing. No pickle is alike, and I had this belief that maybe, one day, I would come across one that I would fall in love with. I would find a pickle that would forever change my perception of them. That day still hasn't come, no matter how many of them I have tried.

The same can't be said for mint chocolate, though. That day, I found one I actually loved. Yes, the chocolate the tour guide gave me made me say the word love. Not tolerate, not the famous words, "I don't like it because it isn't my thing, but I can admit it's good for what it is." *I loved it!*

Cue the imaginary balloons falling from the ceiling! Cue the parade of confetti followed by the mayor presenting me with a sash saying, "Tried again and liked it." That was it!

I was in disbelief, I didn't believe I would ever say, "I love mint chocolate."

Who knew which other things I would be able to fall in love with as well? Solo traveling?

The weirdest part about this story is that you will never know about any of this. You will never know that I changed my stance on one of your favorite flavors. You will never know that my belief of always tasting something, even if I hate it, worked for once, and I found the one. Coming to terms with the fact that I can't share news with you anymore is a hard pill to swallow, no matter how big of a milestone in my journey it is. You simply aren't there anymore, something I'm still mastering how to embrace.

You will never know that, and at the same time, I will never know if you knew what the brand's name meant in Portuguese. The best trade-off. The one where we both lose.

*Hey, we don't believe in card readers, right?*

There is this Spanish saying that I quote all the time, "Yo no creo en brujas, pero que las hay, las hay." It translates to, "I don't believe in witches, but that they exist, they do." I like to use it when talking about supernatural things or things related to astrology and other types of similar arts.

It's a little bit like being agnostic. You want to believe that you have free will, and therefore you reject anything that would say that wasn't true. But you're also unsure if there is an entity or not out there since there is no scientific proof. An entity that would manifest itself through the manipulation of probabilities, such as getting a specific card while reading a tarot deck. In some ways, all of this can be considered as a need for validation, seeking reassurance that you're doing the right thing.

In other words, it's a form of codependency.

I don't seek a card reader to answer the questions that I have. I will say that I'm hesitant to hear what they have to say because I know some parts of it will resonate with me and I will end up hyper-fixating on them.

When I was a kid, while my sister was in college, I had gotten ahold of an oracle deck that she had. It was similar to tarot in the spirit that it provided answers, but it was composed of two decks instead of one. One with zodiac signs, featuring the male and female gender, and the other deck had an action or sentence related to what would happen. One day, I was reading these cards to one of my mother's friends and the cards said that she was going to fall in love with a male Libra. We started laughing since that was my sign, jokingly saying that it was me.

Lo and behold. A few months later, she started dating this man who had the same birthday as me. Different year, though! Still . . . it was indeed a remarkable coincidence.

Around fifteen years later, while I was doing my master's, I was out with a friend drinking, and she dragged me to a palm reader. She had been there before, and it had been such a positive experience that she also wanted me to live it. I didn't have any say in the matter. I was going to end up in that little store getting my palm read whether I wanted to or not.

The lady said the typical generic things, for instance, like I was going to have three kids. But she also said something oddly specific. She mentioned that I would marry my third partner. That had been at a point in my life when I was dating my third boyfriend. It had been odd because that was a low number to say to someone at a young age in a big city. People usually go through several relationships before committing to marriage.

I don't know if my subconscious held those words and tried to make them happen, because the truth is that we did get married. Some could have argued that I manifested it at that time, and the universe granted it to me. My question is, what are manifestations? Asking the universe for something you want, and then working hard to ensure you meet that outcome, no matter how many times you fail, because the universe will eventually give it to you? Isn't this a form of codependency? One where we ultimately get to the end result because of our hard work, but we brush it off, discrediting it, saying that it was a manifestation. That it was intended to happen. In a way, it takes away our power by having us seek external validation. If it failed, it was because the universe didn't want it, not because we didn't try.

That palm reader forgot to tell me something—it wouldn't be a strong marriage. After the two of us decided to get divorced, while I was packing my things to leave our apartment, I dropped a deck of tarot cards. One previous Christmas, I had asked for this *Game of Thrones*-inspired deck because I thought it looked interesting. Even if I never learned how to read the cards, it would still be a charismatic piece of decoration.

I never put much effort into it, and I never learned how to use them. Instead, they just sat inside a drawer until I started packing to leave the apartment I shared with my now-ex. To my surprise, after I dropped all those cards, I noticed that only two were facing up: *Death* and *The Hanged Man*. I quickly investigated the manual to find their meaning as they looked alarming. No one likes to see the *Death* card.

They meant that I was at the end of a cycle and that I had to take one step back in order to take two steps forward. All of that resonated with me a little too much for my liking, so I put the cards back into their box and decided to keep them hidden in my future apartment.

I don't believe in witches, but that they exist, they do. These funny coincidences are either magic or my delusions hyperfixating on the things that resonate with me.

A few weeks ago, out of the blue, I stumbled upon a video on Instagram of a card reader. She said that the viewer was separated from their soulmate and that they were meant to reconnect. She mentioned that this was an intended outcome that needed to happen so both parties could learn and heal.

I shared it with my friends, jokingly saying that the cards were telling me that I should be delusional. Little did I know that it would be a mistake! By sharing it, I fed this information to the algorithm, and suddenly more videos with the same message were everywhere.

I realized that their Instagram pages always featured the same sort of message, one of reconnection, rarely anything else. I thought that it was probably because that's what people want to hear. Someone desperate for reconnection would reach out to them to ask for help, given that the cards told them that they would get what they wanted. They are also seeking validation from someone or something instead of allowing themselves to listen to their inner voice.

People know if something is right or wrong, they just don't want to listen to the voice of reason because it hurts. However, if it's something or someone else saying to run away, then it's easier to detach. They didn't have to make that decision.

I'm in a similar place. I'm slowly detaching from you, but my codependent need for connection was telling me that I should listen to that video. It validated my desire for love. At the same time, all the videos I saw had the same message. It wasn't a coincidence that I saw that one video.

Because of that, I decided to take matters into my own hands and dug out that faithful deck of tarot cards I own. I did a reading with the manual in my hand, and the result was that I was on a journey of improvement and that there was a big challenge in front of me, but I would overcome it and be better off in the end.

Generic! This could have been said about my divorce back then as well. This could also have been said about the mission that I took when I decided to write a book. Or even professionally! Then why did I only interpret this as the relationship challenge that I'm in? I only saw what I wanted to see. The comfort of the validation that we would get back together.

A friend then told me that, if that meant anything, it was that the universe was telling me to go get my cards read by a professional. I thought that there would be no harm in that, but I wouldn't seek one. If I randomly saw a tarot reader one day when I was walking around, then I would go to one. In a way, I was putting this into destiny's hands. If it never wanted me to hear the message, so be it. I'm trying not to be desperate for external validation; instead, I'm learning to give it to myself so I can be happy.

Today, a few weeks after that conversation, I finally saw a card reader who happened to be on the opposite street from where I work. I thought it was interesting how I had walked by that place so many times but never noticed it. I decided to complete my end of the bargain and go inside. The reader laid out the whole deck on the table and started reading every component of my life.

She saw a marriage that wasn't strong. I thought to myself that half of all marriages end in divorce, so it's a safe bet to tell that to anyone, and it wasn't exclusively meant for me.

She also saw three children. The same number the palm reader had said many years before. I brushed it off, thinking that everyone loves that number; three was also the number of partners until marriage.

She then mentioned that I was good in business and with numbers, and that a new opportunity in a more artistic area that I wasn't familiar with would arrive. I would be introduced to it by someone else. At that point, I looked down and thought that my clothes were very casual and that she couldn't easily tell that I worked at an office with numbers. Maybe she was talking about this book! She got me intrigued.

She then said I have never been lucky in love. That she saw that my heart chakra was blocked. However, she could give me healing services and crystals to help with it. I quickly rejected her offer, thinking to myself that this was a scam. My new therapist should be the one healing that chakra, not her.

Lo and behold, she then said exactly what I wanted to hear. The mention of my heart chakra being blocked was for

182

a reason. I had recently met my soulmate and a temporary separation between us was meant to happen so we could both heal, to release the negativity in our lives.

I then entered the realm of confusion. I couldn't figure out which parts were real and which ones weren't. That was oddly specific, and it totally resonated with me. It was also the same messaging as those Instagram videos. At the same time, they only had videos with that message. Is that what everyone wants to hear or was it meant for me?

She mentioned a trip overseas as well, a trip that I was going to take in order to heal. Deep inside, I thought that it was Chicago and I should disregard the overseas part. If I believed in that, I was able to believe in the rest. Believing in that meant that I could start manifesting your return.

Not only did I leave the store feeling confused, but I also felt that I had made a mistake. It was almost like a drug addict having a relapse. I had been fighting so hard to not let the memory of you influence me, but I let it happen today. I sought validation in the cards because I didn't believe my gut feelings that strongly. They are the ones that should tell me if I should fight or run, not some cards.

This journey to fight my codependent tendencies will be a hard one. Luckily, I have a therapist to talk about these things.

I just need to assure myself that I'm okay, and I shouldn't dwell in this fantasy that we were soulmates. That we will reconnect one day. I want to, but I also know it won't be healthy for me. I need to say it: *I'm the maker of my own happiness and destiny.*

# Step Six:

# Repeat

Day ??

*Hey, do you still count the days since we broke up?*

Personally, I will keep counting them as long as you keep visiting me in my dreams. I don't know if it's because I'm writing this book and your memory is always with me or if it's pure love.

What I know is that it's hard to wake up in the morning and start the day already thinking about you. I relive scenarios in my dreams that we once lived—and new fictitious ones. I often wake up wondering if you really texted me in the middle of the night or if it was just a dream. The realization that it was but all a dream, that I won't get the opportunity to see you again, is hard. It's hard because it's the truth.

The truth is also a beautiful thing because it hurts. I'm not the type of person who gets pleasure from pain, but this is different. This hurt shows me how much I cared, how much I appreciated you, and how much I wanted you. I wonder how much longer I should dwell in this misery because in all honesty . . . I'm still uncomfortable with letting the memory of you go. I want to fully detach myself from you, but I can't.

I'm scared that one day I will wake up and go about my day perfectly fine and end it thinking that I don't want or need you anymore. Or that I won't think about you at all anymore. That means I'll be fine without you.

That vision of the future scares me to my core. It would mean that you are irrelevant. I don't want to think that I no longer romanticize our moments. That I no longer fantasize about how it would be nice to cuddle one more time, feeling your body wrapped around mine. I don't want to think that I can be fine without you. I'm fearful of that future, and I still hold onto our memories because of that.

Those memories keep the passion alive, and they remind me of what it's like to love someone so deeply. I relive you repeatedly in those memories. It feels like you are where you should be—with me.

Without these thoughts keeping everything alive, where would all this love go? My guess is that it would create walls around me so I never get hurt again.

I'm still trying to determine when I should stop counting the days and thinking about you. That answer might be when I prevent you from visiting me in my sleep. Then, I will finally be able to stop myself from missing you. One day I will do it when I feel ready because, honestly, today I'm not.

Today, I felt the need to relive it all over again. I wanted to sit on the train ride home after work and imagine all our memories, starting from the day we met. I wanted to recollect the excitement I felt when I was headed to our date. I wasn't counting on crying on the subway. I thought that it had been long enough since we broke up that recalling those moments wouldn't hurt me. But they did.

In between tears, I allowed those memories to come again because I wish things could have worked out. One day, I will realize it's no longer healthy to fantasize about the impossible. One day, I will do it. Today isn't the day.

After the train ride, I walked by a busy street where we once shared so many memories. That was when I looked at one of the Christmas bars we went on a date. I tried to picture us leaving it together, laughing while holding hands. Even though it was out of our way, I still wanted to take you there. It was piled with Christmas decorations and lights, scattered from the roof to the entrance. I had randomly found that bar one night and immediately thought you would love it. I thought that one night, when you were in the area, I had to show it to you.

Today, not a single decoration was in sight, it was a plain uncharismatic bar, a sign that Christmas is long gone. Just like us.

As I kept walking home, I wondered if one day, maybe in five years, I will have to force myself to remember who you are. Will I only remember your existence because I'm talking about how many exes I have had? If that happens, will you be the first one I think of or one of those that I have to think hard to remember? Maybe that will be the point when Christmas will no longer make me think about you.

I don't know the answer to this question. I only know that today I allowed myself to think of you.

Today, I understand that these dreams are unhealthy and bittersweet. I feel pleasure and despair. I want to feel that bliss again. One day, I will stop having these dreams. Today, I allow this desire for happiness to be another impossible daydream that will never happen.

When I got to my apartment, I imagined us spending Christmas together one day in the decorated apartment we would call home. I envisioned you walking through the main door and me rushing to come to you so I could cover your eyes. I would then lead you to the living room to show you the Christmas tree I had put up all by myself. I would take my hands off of your eyes and see a smile on your face. I also imagined the lights reflecting in your eyes, dancing in excitement and joy. I pictured a Christmas tree with new little personalized ornaments that you hadn't seen yet. They represented us and our memories.

A coffee mug that will forever be lukewarm.

A pair of handcuffs.

An arcade.

An ugly Christmas sweater.

A custom figure of us cuddling.

A box of mac and cheese.

A mushroom slice.

A gremlin.

A hammock.

A pickle.

A possum with a Christmas hat on.

A Christmas-themed cocktail glass.

And on top, replacing the star, we would have the one you had already seen: the sparkly Diet Coke ornament I had given to you for Christmas the year that we met.

That was how we started our story. With the comment on Hinge about Diet Coke. The ornament was my first gift to you. It could symbolize a new chapter in our lives once again. Maybe this would have been the moment when I proposed to you. Asking you to spend all the Christmases yet to come together for the rest of our lives.

Today, I know these thoughts aren't healthy, but I allow them. They bring me pleasure through the pain because they show me how much I cared. Tomorrow, I might need to start forgetting about you. One day I will do it.

*Hey, I went back to where it all started.*

I hadn't seen my Coke Zero friend in a while, and we finally made plans to catch up after work today. At last, it was time to bring each other up to date with our lives. Our schedules had been crazy, which didn't give us the opportunity to talk for a while. It didn't help that he went on a long trip to Brazil, and after that, I traveled as well.

As I walked to his apartment, I prepared myself mentally for the conversation about you that would inevitably happen. It happened that my friend and I were both native Portuguese speakers, and it has always felt harder talking about you in my native language, especially with my family.

When I speak Portuguese, it feels like the words cut deeper, as if they have more meaning. The classic example is the word "saudade" where people argue that there is no exact translation to English. I always explain this word as meaning a deeper state of yearning, a profoundly nostalgic longing.

However, this word is barely used in English. The closest English term would be "miss." You miss people but you also miss the train. You miss having a certain food or seeing a person, but you also missed the target. In Portuguese, "saudade" cuts deeper. You don't only miss someone, you yearn for them.

It brings you sadness to live without them, there is melancholy in you. This is also my current state.

When I entered his apartment, I immediately saw a Coke Zero ornament standing there in his entryway. It was almost as if it was mocking me. I had bought him a Coke Zero and you a Diet Coke sparkling ornament that same Christmas. When I saw them, I immediately thought of the two of you, the arch-nemeses of preferences.

I then wondered if you still had yours hanging in your apartment or if you had put it away because it reminded you of me. There is also the possibility that you were able to detach it from any memories of us and the happiness you felt when I gave it to you.

I sat on his couch, talking to him, while deep inside I could only think about the first time you and I talked on that dating app. I was on that exact couch while watching a terrible movie with him. You and I had even joked about bad movies that are so bad they become good by being camp.

The only difference is that back then I was showing my friend my new match. This time I could only say that I had "saudades" of what we had.

I could only think about how many more times this be-havior would end up repeating itself: meeting someone new, opening up, and getting heartbroken. To then meet someone else new, open up again, and end up with another broken heart. And then repeat it all over again. Those thoughts suffo-cated me and made me want to scream. I thought I had found someone who would break this cycle but you happened to just be one more person in this endless loop.

My friend shared the same pain as me. He had stopped seeing a guy due to some incompatibilities between them. Although he was ten years older than me, he was also single and struggling. Seeing all his friends getting married and having kids while he was alone was devastating to him. He talked about how family is so important in our culture. Having a partner makes you not feel like a loser in the eyes of other people. He felt like a disappointment for not having anyone at his age. He was done feeling that way, but he also felt stuck. He couldn't meet anyone for a meaningful relationship.

The weird thing about love is that my friend and I can be two people with similar values and interests, both crying because we are single, but somehow, we don't want to be a couple.

Love isn't about what is easy. It's about that special feeling. It isn't a transaction to prevent two people from dwelling in their loneliness. It's about an attraction and connection that's so rare that it should be treasured whenever it's found.

I was ready to grab this treasure and go around town prancing like a little kid at his school's show and tell, so proud of what I had. You, however, were ready to hide it under your bed like a poorly kept diary with most of its pages missing an entry. You were afraid that showing what you had to others would make it official. You feared that. You dreaded the heartbreak of losing something after showing it to the world.

After that sappy conversation, my friend was fed up. He

dragged me out of the house so we could eat something, get some air, and not dwell on that feeling. While walking to the restaurant, I spotted an interesting flyer promoting an event that got my attention. I knew I would forget about it in five minutes, so, in order to retain its information, I decided to take a photo of it.

Upon taking my phone out of my pocket, I realized something. I finally experienced a feeling I hadn't felt in a long time. I turned to my friend in shock. My eyes were wider than ever. I couldn't believe what was right in front of me.

There was a notification from you on my screen. I couldn't believe my eyes. What did you have to say?

I took a deep breath, trying to gather all the courage required to open the message.

I let out a small squeak, unsure if it was out of fear or excitement. After all this time and everything that has happened to me, my body just froze.

You finally responded to my text, a text I had given up hope of ever seeing a response to. Not only did you agree to let me give you the relationship book I had read, but you also suggested we meet for coffee next Saturday.

Oh, man . . . I'm so nervous for that day . . .

# Acknowledgments

I want to thank all my friends who not only supported me on this literary journey but also provided their shoulders for me to cry on. Thank you.

Thank you, Devon R., for reading my first draft and serving as an honorary line editor. You had a great impact on this book, and now that it's over, I hope you have time to finish your TV shows.

Hi Sean C.! Thank you for reading this piece and providing me with structural edits. "Unhinged lol."

I also appreciate all the constructive feedback I received from beta readers. Not only did it motivate me to publish this piece but it also provided some guidance on how to improve it. Thank you to the fantastic people I found on this journey, especially Alyx R., Andrea Mircheska, Hen Polat, Liz Saucedo, Mary Ellen Kulesa, and Ryan Bailey.

I wouldn't be here if it wasn't for my childhood trauma, so cheers to that.

Lastly, thank you to the person I dedicated this book to. If you made it here, I guess I finished speaking what was on my mind. Over.

www.ingramcontent.com/pod-product-compliance
Lightning Source LLC
Chambersburg PA
CBHW020241130626
46549CB00005B/1995